Practical Solutions for Educating Young Children with High-Functioning Autism and Asperger Syndrome

Practical Solutions for Educating Young Children with High-Functioning Autism and Asperger Syndrome

Mary Jane Weiss, Ph.D.

Foreword by Linda S. Meyer, Ed.D., MPA

Autism Asperger Publishing Company
P.O. Box 23173
Shawnee Mission, Kansas 66283-0173
www.asperger.net

©2008 Autism Asperger Publishing Company
P.O. Box 23173
Shawnee Mission, Kansas 66283-0173
www.asperger.net

Publisher's Cataloging-in-Publication

Weiss, Mary Jane.
    Practical solutions for educating young children with high-functioning autism and Asperger syndrome / Mary Jane Weiss. -- 1st ed. -- Shawnee Mission, Kan.: Autism Asperger Pub. Co., 2007.

       p.; cm.
       ISBN: 978-1-934575-14-7
       LCCN: 2007938303
       Includes bibliographical references and index.

       1. Autistic children--Education. 2. Asperger's syndrome--Patients--Education. 3. Autism in children. 4. Asperger's syndrome in children. 5. Teachers of children with disabilities--Handbooks, manuals, etc. 6. Parents of autistic children--Handbooks, manuals, etc. 7. Parents of children with disabilities--Handbooks, manuals, etc. I. Title.

LC4717 .W45 2007
371.94--dc22   0711

This book is designed in Calcite and Myriad.

Printed in the United States of America.

For four wonderful women,
my forever friends and soul sisters,

Lisa Martin
Jackie Geoghegan
Lynne Stern Feiges
and
Ellen Yeagle

With thanks for blessing me with more joy, support, solace, love,
and laughter than any one person could ever wish or hope for

Acknowledgments

I want to thank all the children with autism spectrum disorders that I have had the privilege to know, and all of their parents, who have trusted me to help their children. It has been an honor to be part of their world and of the autism community.

This book is the result of many years of collaboration with trusted and talented colleagues at the Douglass Developmental Disabilities Center at Rutgers University. First and foremost, I thank my long-time mentors and friends, Dr. Sandra Harris and Dr. Jan Handleman, who started me on this path, who have taught me everything I know about autism and about working with families of children with autism, who have shared their wisdom and experience with me over the years, and who have provided me with encouragement, support, and direction throughout my career. I especially thank Sandy for modeling strength and resiliency, and Jan for modeling diplomacy and compromise. I am forever in their debt.

I would also like to thank my closest colleagues at the center, who have each taught me a great deal over the years: Maria Arnold, Marlene Cohen, Lara Delmolino, Rita Gordon, Marlene Brown, Val Demiri, Barbara Kristoff, Robert LaRue, Donna Sloan, Todd Frischmann, Dania Matthews, Tina Rivera, and Jill Szalony. I especially want to thank Bob LaRue for providing a steady supply of support and humor on a daily basis. Thanks also go to Sharon Grant for keeping track of me and for making it all work.

I am grateful to the people at AAPC who had the vision for this book, and who worked tirelessly with me to see it to its completion. I am especially grateful to Kirsten McBride for her marvelous editing.

On a personal note, I am grateful to my late brother and father, for all the laughter and the memories; to my sister Ruth Anne, brother-in-law Manny, nieces Lisa and Jessica, and my aunt, Ronnie McSweeney, for their unfailing support and love; and to my mother, Joan Rita Coneys, for being an example of excellence, courage, and wisdom to aspire to. I also thank the Weiss family – Pearl, Gerry, Andrea, David, Jake, Jennifer, and Larry – who have given me much support and love over many years. Many thanks go to all of my friends who nurture my soul, especially Lisa, Jackie, Lynne, Ellen, Jon, Mark, Peter, and Suzanne. A special thank you goes to Ilse Gutierrez; nothing would happen without her help – I value her flexibility, camaraderie, and friendship immensely.

From the bottom of my heart, I thank Liam, Nora, and Julia for making my heart dance, and Danny, for being a fine companion and a great refuge through it all.

– M.J.W.

Foreword

How do we begin to address the unique, complicated needs of young learners with high-functioning autism and Asperger Syndrome? This is the question I hear over and over again in parent support groups, schools, conferences, and colleges and universities across the country. Listen:

To the parent: "The places where individuals with Asperger Syndrome are educated extremely well are few and far between." To the teacher: "I have no solid, clinical training in autism spectrum disorders."

To the building administrator: "It's impossible to understand and implement all the modifications needed throughout the school building to accommodate these students."

To the neurotypical peer: "I don't play with Adam; he's boring." To the support staff: "I don't know to help Adam make friends." To Adam: "I tried to tell José that George Washington was the first president of the United States. He ran away and played ball with Sam."

Mary Jane Weiss has heard the questions. She is uniquely qualified to provide the answers. Her professional and research interests have focused primarily on the needs of young learners with autism spectrum disorders and the parents and professionals who support them. Dr. Weiss' most recent text is a readable, practical, systematic roadmap that, when followed, will lead to effective assessment and intervention of young children with high-functioning autism and Asperger Syndrome. Dr. Weiss understands the unique characteristics of these young children who, when they do not receive intensive, systematic instruction, frequently fall through the cracks.

Dr. Weiss has identified and discussed the most important components of an effective and high-quality education and treatment program. Her review of the literature and case scenarios provide examples of the real issues and concerns facing parents and professionals today. This book can not only increase professional competency, it can promote professional compassion. This book can not only increase parents' understanding of their child's needs, it can promote effective advocacy. The result is a blending of professional and parent collaboration leading to socially significant and meaningful change for the youngest learners with high-functioning autism and Asperger Syndrome.

Linda S. Meyer, Ed.D., MPA

Table of Contents

Introduction

Several recent factors have led to an increased number of children with autism spectrum disorders (ASD) being included in typical educational settings. While this offers exciting opportunities for families and their children with ASD, as it provides children with more opportunities for inclusion and integration within their communities, it has also presented numerous challenges. In some cases, school systems have been unprepared to effectively meet the needs of learners with ASD. They may lack the expertise in ASD and in behavioral intervention, they may lack training resources, and they may lack experience in successfully integrating such youngsters into their settings. Families, in turn, have struggled with decisions about what placement is best for their child, given the logistical, training, and expertise challenges that exist in many public school settings.

Increased Numbers in Public Schools

More children with ASD are being identified than ever before. Whereas autism was once considered a low-incidence disorder, recent prevalence and incidence statistics reveal a different story, as ASDs are now estimated to occur in approximately 1 of 150 children (Centers for Disease Control and Prevention; http://www. cdc.gov/ncbddd/autism). There is much discussion and debate about why these numbers are increasing. Certainly, improved diagnostic techniques account for a tremendous portion of that change. Children who were previously missed in classification are now being detected, as our descriptions of ASD have become more thorough and more consistent. It may also be that numbers are actually increasing, for reasons not fully understood. In any case, there are clearly more children receiving diagnoses on the autism spectrum than at any earlier point in time.

Furthermore, those diagnoses are being given at earlier and earlier ages. As a field, we have become more attuned to the manifestations of ASD that occur in infancy and toddlerhood. While it was once the case that delays in language, aberrant social development, or unusual behaviors raised flags for parents and pediatricians, we now look at deviations in development even in preverbal toddlers as possible signs of an ASD. For example, deficits such as failure to point to items or to wave to others are now noted at very early ages. As public awareness of the early signs of ASD has increased, parents have become more vigilant about the development of their children, and pediatricians are increasingly screening for signs of autism routinely at toddler visits. Early intervention programs now treat many children with ASD and young children who are at risk for receiving such diagnoses.

One major benefit of early detection is that intervention is beginning at much younger ages. Many children receive intensive and effective intervention while still extremely young. Unfortunately, there are also many children who receive such diagnoses but do not have access to the most appropriate interventions, or whose levels of treatment fall way below what might produce the best results. There are significant challenges within early intervention systems, especially in terms of how children with ASD are served. Access to services depends on a number of factors, including the state a family lives in and the advocacy skills of a child's parents. Still, early diagnosis increases the chance that intervention begins early and that outcomes may be improved.

In part because of early identification, in part because of the effectiveness of early intensive intervention, children with ASD are also entering the public education system in increasing numbers. By the time many children with ASD reach preschool or kindergarten, they have already received substantial treatment. Whereas children with ASD were often formerly educated in more segregated programs or classrooms, many are now educated in the mainstream educational environment. Thus, general education teachers are encountering many more children with autism than they used to. While many teachers welcome these learners into their classrooms, some experience trepidation. They may ask themselves: Do I have the skills and abilities necessary to help this learner? Do I understand enough about autism to effectively meet this child's needs? How will I help the other students in the class to understand and possibly support this student's challenges? What supports do I need to ask for to be successful as this child's teacher? Who can help me be successful with this learner?

Systems are similarly challenged by this influx of learners with often severe and puzzling needs. Administrators, even if committed to inclusion, may not know what types of supports are essential in helping learners with ASD succeed. Often, service delivery systems are not set up to easily integrate the kinds of training and ongoing team meetings that are necessary to help students on the spectrum. Administrators may struggle with issues of equity, fearing that they are setting precedents that it will be difficult to live up to. They may also be aware that they and their staff lack expertise in how to meet the needs of the population of learners on the autism spectrum, and realize that they need to obtain outside help in creating effective programs for these youngsters.

Challenges Regarding Treatment

It is also sometimes challenging for educators to understand what information they need to learn. There are many schools of thought and treatment approaches to educating children with ASD. There are also many misconceptions about autism and about the treatment of autism. Parents and educators are bombarded with strong opinions about how to teach students with ASD. Many such opinions are presented as facts when, in reality, evidence of their effectiveness is insufficient or entirely lacking.

Perhaps most notably, many parents and educators fail to fully understand which interventions have the best and most robust empirical support. Applied behavior analysis (ABA) is clearly the treatment of choice for individuals on the autism spectrum and is supported by decades of research demonstrating its effectiveness. Nevertheless, some families and professionals fail to appreciate the strong scientific evidence for its effectiveness. Furthermore, they may not understand how seriously lacking in evidence other approaches are.

And even if drawn to ABA, parents may be subject to misinterpretations or misinformation. For example, they may be told that ABA is only relevant for lower-functioning learners or that ABA does not address social deficits. Such views are untrue, but can lead parents to abandon ABA in favor of much less effective interventions. These misconceptions are especially damaging to parents of children with high-functioning autism and Asperger Syndrome (HFA/AS), because they often lead parents to believe that ABA is less relevant for this group of children on the spectrum. As you will see in the chapters of this book, ABA is highly relevant for this group of learners on the spectrum. I have tried to highlight how ABA can be used directly to build social behaviors. Perhaps more important, I have tried to explain how ABA's procedures can be used to integrate other approaches with accountability.

Even when families discover and use ABA to benefit their children, they will likely combine ABA with several other approaches. ABA's emphasis on effectiveness and objectively evaluating the impact of intervention may be its greatest assets. One message of this book is to use what ABA has to offer to evaluate empirically whether and how such approaches are helping a particular child.

Commonly used interventions that lack empirical evidence abound. These include occupational therapy, including sensory integration approaches. Many learners on the spectrum present with very significant sensory challenges, so sensory-based interventions are commonly prescribed. We can use the objective measures and data-based decision making that characterize effective ABA treatment to determine if a particular child is benefiting from such approaches. No parent or educator of children on the spectrum wants to be using procedures that have no value. We need to ensure that what we do with the children we are teaching is working to address their deficits, build their skills, and increase their quality of life.

Similarly, we can use ABA assessment and treatment methods to understand and manage challenging behaviors. In this way, we can ensure that treatment of such behaviors flows from a precise understanding of why an individual is engaging in a particular behavior. We can also ensure that treatment includes strategies to prevent the behavior from occurring, strategies to safely manage the behavior when it does occur, and strategies to teach students alternate, socially appropriate ways to communicate their wants and needs. Furthermore, we can ensure that we do not inadvertently reinforce challenging behaviors by providing reinforcing consequences for behaviors that are not desirable.

Navigating the Maze

At every turn, parents of young children with HFA/AS are faced with challenges. It is challenging to obtain appropriate assessments. Many families even struggle with the diagnosis itself, and encounter differing opinions about how their child's issues can best be described. When a child has HFA or AS, parents may receive even more discrepant opinions about their child, making it more difficult for them to understand just how their child's particular struggles and issues can be best addressed. As mentioned, treatment claims abound. Professionals claim great success, often with little data on the effectiveness of their approach. Furthermore, there is widespread divisiveness within the field about certain approaches, further confusing parents who must make critically important decisions about their child's future.

When children enter school environments, a number of decisions must be made. Teams must outline the educational goals for the particular child and must then decide what type of placement is most appropriate. In order to ensure that the child is successful in a given placement, supports must be provided. In some cases, there may need to be environmental accommodations, such as the use of visual schedules, written directions, or a designated seat near the teacher. Some students may need special motivational systems to provide incentives for engaging in appropriate behavior, for sustaining their attention, and for completing their work. Other students may need the services of a paraprofessional or a shadow to help them respond to the classroom teacher and participate in ongoing classroom lessons. Further, some children require the expertise of a speech therapist, a special educator, or a physical therapist.

Parents need to understand how their child's particular characteristics translate into needs for various kinds of support and assistance. Parents and professionals must work collaboratively to address these needs, to manage conflicting opinions, and to resolve disputes among members of the educational team.

Summary

More children are receiving diagnoses on the autism spectrum, diagnosis is occurring at younger ages, and more children are receiving early intervention services. These realities, combined with a strong value on educating children in the least restrictive environment (LRE), have led to an unprecedented number of children with ASD participating in mainstream educational environments.

At the preschool, kindergarten, and early elementary levels, the needs of learners with HFA/AS are highly variable. Assessment of an individual child's needs is critically important for planning effective treatment. Furthermore, treatment must address the comprehensive needs of each learner. It is a formidable task that requires tremendous planning and the expertise of many professionals. It is my hope that this book will be a useful resource to families as they work to identify their child's needs and to educators as they seek to address those needs effectively.

Chapter 1

UNDERSTANDING STUDENTS WITH HIGH-FUNCTIONING AUTISM AND ASPERGER SYNDROME

JOSHUA was having a difficult time in his preschool classroom. It was hard for him to follow along with the group. He always wanted to be at the train table, building tracks for his favorite Thomas train characters. While he was way ahead of his classmates in many pre-academic skills, he was only interested in demonstrating those skills if they were geared to his interest in trains. He also had a tendency to get extremely upset with little warning, although some triggers for such behavior were predictable. For example, if a child altered the train track or began playing with trains that were not part of Joshua's scenario, he became extremely agitated.

At such times, he might hit the peer. He had also hit the teacher when she intervened in such situations. It was almost impossible to speak calmly with him at these times. His parents were at a loss as to how to help motivate him to behave better and to pay more attention to the teacher.

This chapter will describe the characteristics of preschool children with Asperger Syndrome (AS) and high-functioning autism (HFA). In particular, sensory and learning characteristics, including the need for external reinforcement and the difficulties posed by attentional deficits. The chapter will also review the communication, behavioral, and social characteristics of young learners with AS and HFA, as well as the common challenges they face in school settings.

As is true for all students with autism spectrum disorders (ASD), students with HFA or AS vary widely, and each has particular strengths and challenges. Nevertheless, there are certain common sensory, attentional, learning, and communication difficulties that it is helpful to be aware of. Finally, there are behavioral and social issues that are specific to this population, and that greatly impact upon the learner, peers, and the entire educational community. See Table 1.1 for a summary of characteristics. In the following, we will look briefly at each of these characteristics.

Table 1.1
Summary of Major Characteristics of HFA/AS

SENSORY
> Difficulties with visual and auditory input
>> Distractibility
>> Sensitivity to loud noise
>> Sensitivity to environments with echo
>> Tactile sensitivity
>> Proprioceptive difficulties
>> Vestibular difficulties
>> Hypersensitivity and hyposensitivity

ATTENTION AND LEARNING
> Attention
>> Difficulty coping with group instruction
>> Fixation on details of lesson or materials
>> Difficulty identifying what stimuli to attend to
>> Difficulty following multi-step directions
> Learning
>> Specific learning problems
>> Difficulties in being consistently motivated
>> Specific learning disabilities
>> Difficulties in pre-reading and early decoding skills
>> Listening capacity

COMMUNICATION
>> Difficulty with initiation
>> Passivity
>> Reduced ability to communicate when agitated
>> Lack of reciprocal conversation
>> Excessive discussion on special interest topic
>>> regardless of others' interest
>> Repeated questioning

BEHAVIOR
>> Special interests
>> Need for environmental supports

SOCIAL SKILLS
>> Difficulty creating peer relationships
>> Difficulty initiating, responding to, and comprehending
>>> social situations
>> Interference of special interests

Sensory Issues

Individuals with HFA/AS have a multitude of sensory issues that have been summarized well in other sources (e.g., Moore, 2002; Myles, Cook, Miller, Rinner, & Robbins, 2000; Simpson, 2005). Common problems that impact on school performance include difficulties in dealing with visual and auditory input and difficulties managing a multitude of textures. In addition, there are often difficulties with either hypersensitivity or hyposensitivity across multiple senses. Finally, there can be difficulties in vestibular and proprioceptive functioning.

In the **visual realm**, learners many be overwhelmed by visual stimuli and may have difficulty attending in an environment that is visually busy. They may also be sensitive to certain kinds of visual stimulation, including fluorescent lighting. Some seem to have difficulty with sustaining eye contact, and struggle to visually make or maintain eye contact in situations in which eye contact is socially necessary or expected.

Auditory input can be particularly difficult for students with HFA/AS to deal with, such as sensitivities to loud noises or loud environments. Classic examples include students who panic at the sound of a fire alarm. Other students struggle with the echo or reverberated sounds that occur in bathrooms, gymnasiums, auditoriums, and so on.

Texture difficulties may become apparent in common preschool activities such as finger painting or playing with play dough. That is, some students may not be able to tolerate certain textures on their hands, and may have behavioral difficulties such as tantrums or aggression from extreme anxiety if expected to engage with the material.

BARBARA was making an excellent adjustment to the classroom environment. She followed the classroom routine well, she listened to the teacher consistently, she participated in group instruction, and she was responsive to her peers. However, whenever she left the group environment, things derailed.

The first time it happened was during Community Helper Week. The entire kindergarten grade went to the auditorium, where they met several community helpers, including a police officer, a firefighter, and a doctor. The content of the discussion should have been of great interest to Barbara, as she had been engaged all week within the classroom in topics related to community helpers. However, she was not able to participate in the larger group activity.

The first sign of trouble came after they had just entered the auditorium. She had an immediate negative reaction, and tried to run from the room back to class. The teaching assistant chased after her, brought her back to the auditorium, and tried to calm her. But Barbara became increasingly agitated as the students from other classes filled the room and the ambient noise level increased. Then, the program began, and the helpers began to tell the boys and girls about their jobs. They used a microphone that gave some audible feedback, though nothing that bothered any other learners or staff. Barbara began to tantrum and attempt to exit. She was escorted back to class, where she slowly calmed down.

In talking with her family later, the staff learned that Barbara had had some difficulty in very noisy environments before, including shopping malls and movie theatres.

JOSEPH was very sensitive to different textures. His teachers were aware of it and allowed him to opt out of play-dough and finger-painting activities. It had not occurred to them that he would have difficulty with using a glue border for writing. But when they presented the materials to him, it bothered him on two levels. First he was disturbed by the presence of the border on the paper and immediately tried to remove it. He then became very agitated, as some of the glue stuck to his fingers, and began ripping the paper and threw his chair in frustration.

Difficulties with Attention and Learning

Difficulties with attention and learning are a major part of the struggles for learners with HFA/AS. Often, these difficulties are subtle, and may be manifested in difficult-to-detect ways.

Attention

It is hard for some children with HFA/AS to attend to instructions or to distinguish which parts of instructions are most important. Entering a school environment radically alters the number of environmental factors to attend to (as well as to ignore!). Most children previously have had individual instruction, their experiences with group instruction may be limited and/or their capacity to attend from a distance may be limited. Even students who have been schooled in large groups may have difficulty following directions.

For example, some children with HFA/AS find it difficult to attend to the most *important* aspects of an instructional situation. They may be distracted by aspects of a learning situation that are not relevant to the question. Later, for students in grades K or 1, a transition to an educational environment with a larger number of students presents major challenges.

SALLY was very interested in the little teapot book. She became fixated on acting out the song (putting herself into the handle and spout positions, repeating pages over and over again). She got agitated when the teacher wanted to sing the song straight through, wanting instead to focus repeatedly on the pages with the spout and handle language.

ALEX was good at paying attention during circle time. However, if the screensaver on the computer was within his view, he was drawn to it and found it difficult to hear or see anything else going on in the classroom.

Students with HFA/AS may also have difficulty following directions that consist of several steps. For example, they may be able to attend only to short segments of instruction, they may respond only to the first part of a series of instructions, or they may be delayed in their responses to sequenced instructions. This makes it difficult for them to keep up in a classroom environment in which a *series* of instructions is commonly delivered.

For some learners, the modality of instruction also matters. For example, if directions are given only verbally, it may be more difficult for the student to follow them. Many students with HFA/AS can engage in multi-step tasks with some supports such as textual instructions, picture cues, or sequenced reminders.

STEPHEN had trouble following directions in his kindergarten class-room. He usually could do the first part of the direction, but then became confused or unfocused. At these times, he often began wandering around the room. His teacher changed the way she delivered instructions to the whole class, incorporating visual cues for each step of a given task. The instructional assistant would also provide a mini visual chart of the steps of the assignment and place it on Stephen's desk. If Stephen got distracted, the teacher or aide could then direct him either to the class chart or to his own miniature version of it.

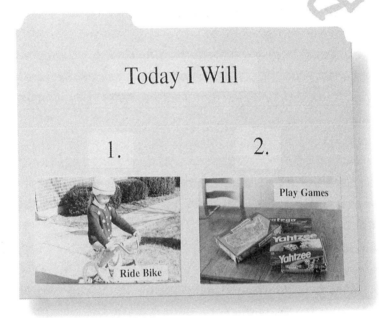

Learning

While learning may not be the major concern among students with HFA/AS, it usually presents significant challenges. Thus, while rote learning is usually a considerable strength, and while there may be areas of strength above age level, there are inevitably areas of significant weakness. At times, strengths obscure needs, leading teachers to "miss" areas of deficit. For example, a learner may read beautifully but may have significant comprehension deficits.

Common types of learning challenges include difficulties in areas of relative weakness (e.g., areas that are much weaker than their overall skill level), difficulties in being consistently motivated to learn, and the presence of specific learning disabilities.

Difficulties in areas of relative weakness may require the development of compensatory strategies or an emphasis on utilization of strengths. For example, a student who has difficulty with auditory attending might be helped by the provision of written directions. Similarly, a student who has difficulty with recalling information for tests might be helped by providing tests that require only recognition of key words or ideas.

Difficulties with being consistently motivated to learn can be an issue for all learners, but is often of particular concern for students with HFA/AS. Often, these students have difficulty when the subject matter is not of intrinsic interest to them. They may also have difficulty sustaining attention and may engage in off-task behaviors. As a result, they may need special incentives for remaining on task during certain activities.

MICHAEL was very interested in science and loved learning about the solar system and about plants. However, he had no interest in things like identifying colors and making letters. During non-preferred activities, Michael often stared out the window or drew pictures of the planets. His teacher knew that he really liked a certain planet computer game. Using this special interest, she developed a motivational system so Michael could earn access to the game. If Michael got stars during all his classroom activities (5 for the morning), he could have 15 minutes to play the planet computer game before lunch.

Whenever **specific learning disabilities** *are present,* special attention should be given to remediating them. As mentioned, the cognitive abilities of many children on the higher end of the autism spectrum sometimes obscure the existence of learning problems. It is important to identify and treat any learning disability. Indeed, behavioral difficulties often improve remarkably when such problems are addressed. In Chapter 2 we will discuss assessment in detail.

Difficulties with Communication

Communication is an area of deficit for all children on the autism spectrum. Children with HFA/AS may have well-developed vocabularies and good superficial communication abilities, but they are often not able to communicate effectively in social contexts. For example, they may not be able to assert themselves with peers, initiate to others, understand figurative language or humor, or grasp the subtle social messages embedded in the communication of others.

Also, while vocabulary knowledge may be a strength, there may be differences between expressive and receptive language skills that are sometimes difficult to detect. Thus, students with well-developed language skills still often struggle to communicate effectively in school.

One major deficit is in the realm of *initiating*. Many students with HFA/AS do not spontaneously request items that they want or need, or communicate without being instructed to do so. Such students may become proficient at responding to others, but not necessarily at navigating their environments. That is, they may await instructions or cues from others that they may request needed items (Cardon, 2007).

Such passivity is worrisome, especially for environments with larger student:teacher ratios where learners' needs might be ignored while the teacher is busy attending to other matters. In recent years, much more emphasis has been placed on teaching requesting skills to students with ASD, because such skills are essential to independent functioning in all environments (e.g., Partington & Sundberg, 1998; Sundberg & Partington, 1998). While the needs of students with HFA/AS might not clearly include this skill deficit, it should be considered as part of a comprehensive assessment and intervention program. It is certainly true that passivity and low rates of initiation characterize students with HFA/AS as well (e.g., Moore, 2002).

There are serious consequences to failing to initiate. Many individuals with HFA/AS suffer greatly from anxiety in social contexts and avoid interacting to prevent reprimand, embarrassment, and discomfort. Many quietly struggle without requesting assistance, simply waiting for others to notice their needs or offer them help. For example, a student who does not understand a given direction may wait for the teacher to notice his failure to comply. Many times, this deficit is due both to deficiencies in initiation and social anxiety. Many socially anxious children react strongly to even a mild redirection. It is definitely the case that social anxiety can inhibit communication.

Perhaps most important within the area of communication, some children with HFA/AS are not able to use all their language skills at all times. For example, they may fail to use language when anxious or angry, instead engaging in disruptive behavior. Often, students with HFA/AS need extra supports to help them communicate effectively when they are agitated. Many students respond well to the use of cards that they can use to communicate when vocal language fails them (to request a break or to ask to speak to a teacher following an upsetting incident, for example).

In addition, there are students with HFA/AS who "order others around" in play. Their play lacks the back-and-forth reciprocity that is typically seen in children. While it may look like initiation, their behavior is more a manifestation of rigidity or scripting. Children who engage in this type of play often appear to be treating others as objects; the message is "do this because I say so."

Students with HFA/AS experience "meltdowns" (Myles & Southwick, 2005), and these eruptions are often associated with a significantly diminished capacity to express feelings or desires. Generally, demand for verbal expression exacerbates the emotional upset. In these circumstances, it is important to work on calming the child and reestablishing stability.

It is essential that staff members recognize that the student is not willfully out of control, oppositional, or non-compliant at these times. The student has simply become so agitated that calming becomes the prime objective. Calming techniques that may work especially well in such instances include deep breathing or special relaxation strategies. However, it is important that teachers ensure that they are not inadvertently reinforcing the behavior.

SEBASTIAN had made a fairly good adjustment to his integrated preschool setting. The teachers were working hard to help him adapt flexibly to all the demands, but he had difficulty when things were unpredictable or when he had to change his schedule or wishes.

It was time for play centers, and everyone at the center was playing in the kitchen. Two of the other students were pretending to make pancakes for breakfast. Sebastian wanted it to be lunch preparation, because breakfast had already happened.

The teacher intervened, trying to distract Sebastian. Sebastian became tearful and upset, and then he began flinging his limbs about. He emptied the carton of kitchen prop toys all over the carpet, and began screaming and violently kicking the toy kitchen. The teacher calmly helped him to a quiet corner of the room and to a beanbag chair. She did not speak too much, but put on some preferred music to calm him. Later, they practiced counting and breathing deeply to further calm him. Finally, he was made to restore the environment by cleaning up the mess he had made and to tolerate some kitchen play before joining classroom activities.

Difficulties with Behavior

Many students with HFA/AS are highly preoccupied with special interests. Such interests may be stereotypical, or repetitive and nonfunctional. For example, a child may like lining up toy cars in a perfect row under the bookcase. Alternately, some children exhibit special interests that are highly unusual or ritualized. For example, a child may be interested in trains to an excessive degree. He may be unwilling to play with any other materials in the classroom. He may be unwilling to respond to a teacher or peer unless addressed as Thomas (the tank engine) or as one of

Thomas' friends. Such special interests may make children unresponsive to other kinds of instruction, making it difficult for them to focus on tasks presented to them or to modulate the level of interest they have in certain topics.

They may also engage in very rigid or inflexible routines or rituals that can be difficult to interrupt. They may have difficulty tolerating disarray in the environment, or a change in the set-up of the physical environment. They may engage in repetitive motor mannerisms. All of these behavioral characteristics predispose learners with HFA/AS to behavioral challenges, as they become upset when access to their interests or routines is limited or altered in some way.

Careful assessment of the maintaining factors associated with the challenging behaviors is critical to comprehensive intervention. Much can be done to prevent behavioral difficulties by creating a supportive environment through appropriate and tailored accommodations. Furthermore, students can be taught a variety of communicative and other skills to more efficiently get their needs met. These will be further explored in Chapters 3 and 4.

ANDREW was very interested in the Power Rangers. This was an asset with peers. He often brought Power Ranger characters to Show and Tell, and he was known as a resource among peers about the Rangers. He could provide facts on each color Ranger, and he knew each episode by heart. At Halloween time, he and several other boys in the class decided together to be Power Rangers, each dressing up as his favorite character.

The teachers and Andrew's parents were delighted to have such an easy social bridge for enhancing conversation and play between their son and his peers. However, Andrew's interest in the Power Rangers began to become excessive and hard to redirect. Both at home and in school, he began taking on the persona of rangers, wanting to be "in character" for most of the day. In fact, he wanted to be addressed as a Power Ranger. If he was referred to as Andrew, he would correct his conversational partner, saying, "I am not Andrew. I am the Red Power Ranger." At first, both his family and his teachers indulged him, as it seemed to lead to prolonged conversations, high levels of imaginative play, and high-quality engagement. Andrew seemed animated and enthusiastic when interacting as a Power Ranger.

All of these were deemed very positive developments. Soon, however, Andrew would tantrum if someone insisted on interacting with "Andrew." He refused to discuss other topics. He made every assignment in class Power Ranger-related, inserting details on the Power Rangers into his journal and drawings. Even his peers became wary of his interest in the Power Rangers, as Andrew got more controlling of the play scenarios and conversations about the Rangers. Eventually, peers began to reduce their level of contact with him.

TARA was a very attentive and engaged student and an excellent listener. She was exceptionally good at cleaning up after play time or centers. She knew where every item went, and she was usually the first student to respond to the cue to clean up. She was sometimes very rigid about how items got put away. Some of the students in the class put blocks away more haphazardly than she did. For example, they might place them all fairly randomly on the blocks shelf, whereas Tara stacked them in order of height. It disturbed her when other children were at the block center and put the blocks away in a manner that differed from her preferences.

*The teacher tried to distract Tara from her concern, but was not suc-
cessful. Tara would dart across the room to ensure that the blocks
were being put away "correctly." If she was prevented from doing
this, she continued to be focused on the disarray, and remained agitated into the next activity. She even left subsequent activities and
centers to go back and fix the blocks.*

Difficulties with Socialization

Students with HFA/AS usually have difficulty in developing peer
relationships. The issues that exist for many of these students
are slightly different from those that exist for other learners
on the autism spectrum, though some are shared. One of the
things that sometimes make it hard for children with HFA/AS
(compared to more impaired students with classic features of
autism) is that they do not appear to be as obviously disabled. In
other words, others may not understand the nature or severity
of their struggles to learn, communicate, and integrate, because
they have many well-developed skills. However, they do struggle,
often mightily, and nowhere more significantly than in social relationships.

Many students with HFA/AS do not seek to include or draw the
attention of others to themselves or their activities. This can
result in isolation, and can impede the establishment of social
connections. Even their ability to respond to the social bids of
others is highly variable. While some students are more adept
than others at this kind of give-and-take, most struggle when circumstances become less interesting to them, more abstract and
emotionally charged, or when interaction is required for longer
durations.

It is also difficult for students with HFA/AS to interpret and respond to the nonverbal communication of others. These difficulties often make it difficult for them to understand or function effectively in social situations, and they may hit roadblocks with their peers even when they are interested in them. If they do initiate to peers, their bids may be ineffective, lacking clarity or appropriateness. While they may be very interested in joining a group, they may not be effective at conveying that interest.

An issue specific to children with HFA or AS is their unusual interests and abilities, as mentioned earlier. That is, they may be unable to relate to the interests of their peers, and their peers may find their interests difficult to comprehend.

ETHAN was a very smart preschooler who excelled in all pre-academic tasks. He was quiet and withdrawn most of the time. However, he had a few interests he was very passionate about, and he would initiate to peers about them. For example, he loved facts about the U.S. presidents. He knew all of the presidents, when they served, and several facts about each. He often initiated to peers by talking about presidents.

His peer group was unfamiliar with the presidents, aside from (in some cases) knowing the name of the current president. Ethan was sometimes frustrated by the lack of response or interest from peers. He often relied on attention to the facts from his teacher, who had mixed feelings about engaging him on a topic that was not helping to bridge the social gap with his peers.

MATTHEW was a bright kindergartner who was largely indistinguishable from his peers, except in terms of his great intellect. He was struggling socially with his friends, who were very interested in trading Pokémon cards. He expressed to his parents that he thought Pokémon cards were dumb, and he couldn't believe that kids wanted to spend so much time talking about them. His teacher and parents wondered whether they should encourage him to embrace the Pokémon phenomenon or let him develop interests of his own (even if it led to more social isolation).

BILLY was very interested in Thomas the Tank Engine. His parents were hopeful that it could be a bridge to making connections with other kids. After all, many preschool boys like trains. At preschool, there was a train table set up in the classroom. Billy always wanted to be there. If he was made to go to another center, he simply looked at and talked about trains. When he was at the train center, he wanted to play alone, and he had very specific ideas about how he wanted to play. Most often, he wanted to enact a scene from a favorite movie about trains. When his friends wanted to do something different, he had a tantrum.

Dilemmas such as those illustrated on the preceding pages are not uncommon. It is a difficult balance to nurture special interests and to guide social integration. Ideally, as educators and parents, we would like to do both. We do not seek to squelch the individuality and interests of the child, and we want to help prevent the pain that can come with social rejection. A variety of strategies can be used to streamline the intensity of these interests, to expand the capacity for and breadth of social contact, and to help build a community of friends with similar interests. These will be explored in Chapter 3.

Common Challenges

Young students with HFA/AS encounter a variety of common challenges in school. The characteristics discussed above predispose them to a host of difficulties in meeting the demands of teachers and peers, as well as work requirements. It is often difficult for them to tolerate the wide variety of sense experiences that bombard them. This is an important aspect of the school experience that should not be overlooked, and a very important dimension of assessment for an individual learner. Attentional and learning challenges are sometimes obscured, in the face of great intellectual strengths and assets. Nevertheless, it is important to identify specific individual challenges that may exist in these realms.

Communication difficulties are also very prevalent and can interact with and predispose the child to intense behavioral reactions. Social difficulties can create isolation, withdrawal, and fear of rejection. Social anxiety is an often-unrecognized aspect of social functioning, and needs to be addressed to help the learner function more effectively in group learning environments.

Summary

This chapter has given a flavor of some of the common themes and issues related to educating young students with HFA/AS. However, the ways in which these characteristics manifest themselves are as variable as each child is from another. While it is important to recognize that there are themes and common vulnerabilities, it is equally important to realize that each child is an individual, and that one can only understand how to help an individual learner by getting to know that individual learner very well.

In the coming chapters we will be examining assessment and intervention strategies that can be tailored to meet the needs of each unique learner. We will also review strategies for creating effective teams and for planning for successful transition experiences.

Chapter 2

ASSESSMENT

Assessment is of central importance for success in educating learners with AS and HFA, yet much confusion exists about ways to meaningfully assess this population of learners. Assessment of preschool children with AS and HFA is a multidimensional process. With some learners, it may be necessary to assess aspects of autism itself, such as the ways in which social deficits are expressed. It may also be useful to assess cognitive skills, specific skill areas, play and social skills, and language use.

Standardized tests may fail to accurately identify the strengths and weaknesses of children with HFA/AS, and may inadequately inform educators about important potential goals. Instruments such as Stanford Binet Intelligence Scales, 4th edition (Thorndike, Hagen, & Sattler, 1986) and the Wechsler scales (the Wechsler Intelligence Scale for Children [WISC-III; Wechsler, 1991] and the

Wechsler Preschool and Primary Scale of Intelligence Revised [WPPSI-R; Wechsler, 1989]) can be highly relevant in outlining areas of strength and weakness, but pose difficulties for some learners (e.g., timed tasks, knowledge of specific content). Thus, these instruments may need to be supplemented with other assessments of specific skills.

Further, even in fluent verbal learners, it may still be necessary to assess how they use their language abilities in natural contexts. For example, it may be useful to use narratives (verbal and/or written) to assess language use. Issues such as conversational skills (topic management, shifting topics, ending conversations), clarification skills, interpretation of nonliteral language, and the capacity to match communication to context and listener are often challenging for this population, yet very important as they are highly relevant to how the individual will function in a classroom environment and in peer interactions.

Play and social skills are also important in young learners. Play is a bridge to social connections with others, and aberrant play can be stigmatizing and may result in isolation. Assessment of these skills is important as a comparison to age peers and for identifying teaching goals.

Ways to assess behavior and motivation have substantially improved in recent years. Educators must identify why children are engaging in challenging behaviors and what will serve to effectively motivate them. Accommodations can be made to prevent behaviors from occurring, and replacement skills take the place of less functional behaviors. Furthermore, a well-motivated student will not only learn more efficiently, but will also be more cooperative and less disruptive.

Finally, it is important to assess the sensory realm for students on the autism spectrum. For example, it may be possible to develop hypotheses that lead to interventions that increase comfort. This usually results in improvements in behavior as well.

This chapter will examine a variety of areas in which assessment is important, and will discuss the relevance of a variety of different assessment tools in each domain. Specifically, we will discuss how to assess autism symptoms, skills and abilities, play and social skills, and behavior and motivation (see Table 2.1).

Table 2.1
Potential Areas to Assess in Young Children with AS and HFA
• **Autism symptoms**   • **Skills and abilities**   • **Play and social skills**   • **Behavior and motivation**   • **Sensory issues**

Autism Symptoms

Diagnosis may have been clarified by the time the child with HFA/AS enters school, but many children are identified during the early years of school. Even if the child has received a diagnosis, educators may still be trying to determine whether a child is on the autism spectrum, or whether her difficulties are better explained by other disabilities. In some cases, it is difficult for the clinician to determine if HFA/AS is the best descriptor. Other commonly considered diagnoses include learning disabilities, attention deficit hyperactivity disorder (ADHD), obsessive-compulsive disorder, and oppositional-defiant disorder.

It is sometimes difficult to separate the behavioral and other features of autism spectrum disorders (ASD), and it may take several years to get the best and most accurate diagnosis. However, in recent years, great progress has been made in diagnosing ASD. In particular, the Autism Diagnostic Interview (AD; Lord, Rutter, & LeCouteur, 1994), the Autism Diagnostic Interview-Revised (ADI-R; LeCouteur, Lord, & Rutter, 2001), and the Autism Diagnostic Observation Scale (ADOS; Lord, Rutter, DiLavore, & Risi, 2001) are excellent and reliable instruments for identifying children on the spectrum. However, they may be better at identifying classical autism and pervasive developmental disorders-not otherwise specified, and may be less useful for HFA and AS. Nevertheless, is particularly helpful to use these instruments to screen for deficits in joint attention, imaginative play, use of language in social contexts, and conversational ability.

Autism Diagnostic Interview-Revised

The ADI is an in-depth, semi-structured parental/caregiver interview. Focusing on the child's social relatedness, communication abilities, and repetitive behaviors, the interview determines diagnosis and level of severity. The interview takes between 90 minutes and 3 hours to administer. Parents are asked highly specific questions about their child's early language and social development and about current language, social, and behavioral skills. Table 2.2 lists sample ADI items.

Table 2.2
Sample Items from the ADI

RECIPROCAL CONVERSATION
Can you have a conversation with _____? That is, if you say something to him/her without asking a direct question, what will _____ usually do?

SOCIAL SMILING
When _____ is approaching someone to get them to do something or to talk to them, does he/she smile in greeting?

CIRCUMSCRIBED INTERESTS
Does he/she have any hobbies/interests that are unusual in their intensity?

Autism Diagnostic Observation Scale

The ADOS, an observational instrument, is a companion tool to the ADI. Using this scale, the child is asked to do a series of tasks with the examiner in the presence of a parent. This brief (30 minutes to 1 hour) activity often sheds light on specific deficits that can create social difficulties and can help in developing goals in the social and speech realms. Tasks assess for imaginative play, joint attention, social engagement, and the social use of language.

There are four modules of the ADOS to choose from based on the participant's chronological age and expressive language abilities. The activities in each module are designed to be interesting and to provide natural opportunities for social and communicative behaviors to occur. The assessment is usually very enjoyable and engaging for the learner, and parents are encouraged to join their child in several of the activities. Table 2.3 lists sample items from the ADOS.

Table 2.3
Sample Items from the ADOS

BUBBLE PLAY
Task: Instructor activates a bubble machine and awaits child's response.

Goal: Observe child's behavior while bubbles are present. Especially focus on initiation of joint attention in order to share interest and pleasure.

ANTICIPATION OF A ROUTINE
Task: Instructor blows up a balloon and lets it fly across the room. Instructor repeats activity several times.

Goal: Observe child's affect, initiation of joint attention, shared enjoyment, requesting, and behavior.

BIRTHDAY PARTY
Task: Instructor brings out a doll and says it is the doll's birthday. Instructor makes a cake with play dough, and has candles and dishes available to enact a party.

Goal: Observe child's ability to join in the script of a birthday party. Especially observe for participation in and contributions to enactment of party, imitation of instructor's actions, and whether doll is treated representationally.

In addition to its use for early diagnosis, there has been preliminary interest among clinicians and researchers in using the ADOS as a measure of change for children with ASD. As many of the activities assess for skills such as joint attention, requesting, social referencing (e.g., looking at a parent to share an experience or see a reaction) and communication, it may be possible to look for changes in children's social and communicative behavior over time. This is an interesting possibility, as it may be possible to see progress in social and communicative realms over time with repeated administrations of the ADOS.

EMILY came to the session interested and happy, and seemed to settle in well to the activities in the ADOS. She enjoyed many of the tasks presented and even seemed to like the examiner, smiling at her a few times. After the assessment, the examiner explained to Emily's parents that their daughter met the criteria for autism. The examiner noted her strengths and her interest in the activities and in the examiner, but also pointed out that Emily did not seek to share her enthusiasm with her parents (who were in the room). And while she had spoken, her phrases were routinized, her language was never paired with eye contact, and she hadn't been able to keep a conversation going with the examiner. Her parents could see how these deficits affected their daughter, and conveyed their anxiety to the examiner that others expect more of her because her language and skills are so well developed.

Questionnaires and Other Screening Tools

In addition to the observational and interview instruments described above, several questionnaires are also available as screening tools for autism. These tools are not designed to be used in isolation for the diagnosis of autism, but can be useful in screening for problems on the autism spectrum.

Gilliam Autism Rating Scale (GARS; Gilliam, 1995). This is a behavioral checklist that can be completed by parents or professionals. It contains autism-specific content in the areas of communication abilities, socialization abilities, and stereotyped behaviors, and it contains questions about the child's development during the first three years of life. The resulting score indicates the probability that the child has autism and the severity of the autism. It can be used with participants ages 3 years to 22 years old.

Autism Behavior Checklist (ABC; Krug, Arick, & Almond, 1980). This checklist of behavioral characteristics common in the diagnosis of autism can be filled out by parents or teachers. It contains descriptors in five areas: sensory, relating, body and object use, language, and social and self-help skills.

Checklist for Autism in Toddlers (CHAT; Baron-Cohen, Allen, & Gillberg, 1992). This is a tool designed for early detection of autism at 18 months by pediatricians. It contains interview questions for parents to endorse as well as brief observational probes. Nine developmental areas cover such critical issues as pretend play, proto-declarative pointing, and joint attention. The CHAT has utility in predicting at 18 months those children who later are diagnosed with autism and those who are not (Baron-Cohen et al., 1992; Baron-Cohen et al., 1996).

Skills and Abilities

Children with HFA/AS will be assessed many times and by many professionals. The goal of such assessments is to help identify strengths and areas of relative weakness and to develop goals that are relevant and meaningful for the learner. Assessments can also be used to highlight discrepancies from same-age peers, which is also very relevant for identification of appropriate goals.

Types of assessments for young children commonly include assessments of cognitive ability, adaptive behavior, and school-relevant skills such as group-instruction skills, play skills, and social skills. Many children also receive assessments specific to maximizing their performance (motivation assessment) or understanding behavioral challenges (functional assessment). In addition, some children benefit greatly from a sensory assessment. In any sound and responsible testing situation, examiners do their utmost to ensure the most representative results as discussed under Testing Considerations.

Testing Considerations

Sometimes, young children have difficulty performing tasks for an unfamiliar examiner. As a result, often after listening to a report of their child's performance, parents comment that their child could have done a particular activity described as not being performed on the test, or have done it better than in the testing situation.

Examiners will try to get a sense of whether a child's performance is typical and do everything they can to maximize performance. At times, they may invite a parent or a known and familiar educator to the assessment to increase the child's comfort level. They may also inquire about a particular motivational system or item that might enhance and sustain the child's attention and motivation. For example, they may bring the child's sticker chart into the session or contract with the child for a favorite snack at the session's end.

Cognitive Abilities

Every child with special needs is given an assessment of cognitive ability (i.e., an intelligence test), often initially at diagnosis, when entering the educational system, and then on a regular basis (e.g., every 2 to 3 years). These tests yield a great deal of information about tasks and activities a student can do well and things that he or she finds challenging. Often students with HFA/AS do well on such tests because of their high innate intelligence. Nevertheless, they still face challenges. Many of them struggle with the unfamiliarity of the examiner or of the materials, as discussed above.

Furthermore, many students with ASD struggle with the demands of standardized tests. For example, standardized tests require the examiner to ask the questions in one, and only one, way for the results to be reliable. Flexibility in how tasks are administered or in the language used in instruction is not permitted. Furthermore, most of the tests require that the student be given a number of items that they do not pass in order to complete the assessment. This can be frustrating, especially for a learner with a low tolerance for difficult or novel tasks. In particular, students with HFA/AS often struggle with the language demands and the need for sustained attention during standardized tests. The use of timed tests also poses difficulty for learners who require more time to execute their responses.

It is essential that testing conditions be arranged to maximize student performance and minimize anxiety. First, great attention should be given to developing rapport. This is essential to ensure that the sample of performance is the student's best effort. Examiners need to take time to engage the student in play or in conversation about preferred items and activities. Further accommodations may include a non-standardized administration (e.g., not timing performance, altering language of instructions). Such changes may improve performance, but the danger is that it may alter the administration in a way that reduces the validity and utility of the results. In other words, the results from non-standardized administration describe the learner's skills and abilities in a more comprehensive way, but are no longer comparable to others of the same age as they would be if the test were given in the standardized way.

Common modifications are listed in Table 2.4 below. Some changes do not alter the administration of the test and are simply designed to accommodate the special needs of the learner. Other changes may necessitate scoring the test differently from how it was designed to be scored. (In Table 2.4, these changes are indicated with an asterisk.) In these cases, the clinician may report scoring in both the traditional and modified formats.

Table 2.4 *Common Test Modifications*	
DIFFICULTY	**ALTERATION/MODIFICATION**
Nonpreferred/unfamiliar tasks	• Intersperse with preferred material • Use reinforcers • Use token system
Novel environments	• Test in a familiar environment
Novel instructors	• Have familiar teacher or parent present
Sustained, in-seat work	• Break testing up into several sessions
Hard tasks	• Provide a break card • Allow student to opt out as needed • Do not approach ceilings (*)
Working quickly	• Do not time performance (*)
Comprehending instructions	• Alter instructions (*) • Pair with familiar instructions (*) • Prompt response (*) • Model answer (*)

One of the positive outcomes of a cognitive assessment is that it leads to an understanding of relevant strengths and deficits, which, in turn, helps teachers develop appropriate and realistic expectations in all areas of performance. It may also help staff members understand a student's frustration with particular activities that require skills that are relative weaknesses for the student.

Common cognitive assessment instruments used include the Stanford Binet Intelligence Scales, 4th edition (Thorndike et al., 1986) and 5th edition (Roid, 2003); the Kaufman Assessment Battery for Children (K-ABC; Kaufman & Kaufman, 1983); the Wechsler Intelligence Scale for Children (WISC-III; Wechsler, 1991) and the Wechsler Preschool and Primary Scale of Intelligence Revised (WPPSI-R; Wechsler, 1989); and the Different Abilities Scale (Elliot, 1990). Any of these scales may be appropriate for a given learner, and an experienced examiner should be able to make an appropriate choice, based on information such as that listed in Table 2.5.

CHARLIE was struggling in school in a number of areas, so his team decided to do some cognitive testing to help identify areas of strength and areas of weakness. While they found that Charlie had exceptional visual memory skills and excellent visual-spatial skills, they also discovered that verbal memory and verbal reasoning skills were weak.

They began to offer more visual supports to Charlie across the day. They focused particularly on the provision of a visual schedule, on visual cues to complete multi-step tasks, and on presenting feedback in concrete and visual ways such as via signals and cards. They also began to monitor themselves for excessive verbal instruction to cue themselves to provide instructions in more visual ways. Finally, they began to use a visual timer to help Charlie to anticipate the amount of time left in activities and to help prepare him for transitions.

Table 2.5
Examples of Instruments Used for Cognitive Assessment

INSTRUMENT	AGE RANGE	UNIQUE MEASUREMENT FEATURES
Stanford Binet, 4th ed.	2.5 to adult	Assesses • Verbal reasoning • Abstract/visual reasoning • Quantitative reasoning • Short-term memory
Stanford Binet, 5th ed.	2.5 to adult	Assesses • Fluid reasoning • Knowledge • Working memory • Visual-spatial processing • Quantitative reasoning

Wechsler Scales
   WPPSI-R
   WISC-III
	3 to 7
	6 to 16 years
		Provides verbal and performance IQ scores
		Provides verbal and performance IQ scores

K-ABC	2.5 to 12.5	Sequential processing assessment Simultaneous processing assessment • Emphasizes spatial skills Achievement scales for reading & math
DAS	2.5 to 17	Early preschool section Late preschool section School-aged section Assesses • Verbal reasoning • Nonverbal reasoning (spatial)

Adaptive Behavior

An assessment of adaptive behavior is often done along with a cognitive assessment. Adaptive behavior assessments focus on independence and mastery in a variety of domains relevant to everyday life, including motor skills, communication, self-help skills, and socialization. Some instruments yield age-equivalent scores that indicate the developmental levels achieved in each area.

A number of measures of adaptive behavior are available. Most are administered via interview with a parent or a checklist that is completed by a parent or teacher; or sometimes both.

The Vineland Adaptive Behavior Scales (Sparrow, Balla & Cicchetti, 1984; recent revision: Vineland-II; Sparrow, Cicchetti, & Balla, 2005). This instrument, typically administered as an interview, has been shown to be sensitive to changes over time when used with individuals with ASD (Harris, Handleman, Belchic, & Glasberg, 1995). The Vineland-II assesses skills in several key areas, as listed in Table 2.6. (Sample items are also listed.)

Table 2.6
Areas Tested and Sample Items from Vineland-II

COMMUNICATION
Receptive
- Points to at least 3 major body parts when asked
- Follows instructions with one action and one object
- Follows instructions in "if-then" form
- Follows three-part instructions

Expressive
- Points to object he/she wants that is out of reach
- Says at least 50 recognizable words
- Tells about experiences in simple sentences
- Asks questions beginning with who or why

Written
- Recognizes own name in printed form
- Copies own first name
- Identifies all printed letters of the alphabet (upper and lower case)
- Prints or writes own first and last name from memory

DAILY LIVING SKILLS
Personal
- Drinks from a cup or glass, may spill
- Pulls up clothing with elastic waistband
- Asks to use toilet
- Wipes or blows nose using tissue or handkerchief

Domestic
- Is careful around hot objects
- Helps with simple household chores
- Cleans up play/work area at end of activity
- Clears unbreakable items from own place at table

Community
- Demonstrates understanding of function of telephone
- Talks to familiar person on telephone
- Counts at least 10 objects, one by one
- Is aware of and demonstrates appropriate behavior while riding in car

---

Table 2.6 (cont.)
SOCIALIZATION

SOCIALIZATION

Interpersonal Relationships
- Shows interest in children the same age
- Imitates simple movements
- Shows desire to please others
- Answers when familiar adults make small talk

Play and Leisure Skills
- Chooses to play with other children
- Shares toys or possessions when asked
- Uses common household objects or other objects for make-believe activities
- Plays simple make-believe activities with others

Coping Skills
- Changes easily from one at-home activity to another
- Says thank you when given something
- Changes behavior depending on how well he or she knows another person
- Ends conversations appropriately

MOTOR SKILLS

Fine
- Removes object from a container
- Turns pages of a book one at a time
- Stacks at least 4 small blocks or other small objects
- Opens doors by turning doorknobs

Gross
- Kicks ball
- Throws ball of any size in specific direction
- Catches beach-ball sized ball with both hands from a distance of 2-3 feet
- Walks up stairs alternating feet (may use rail)

It is particularly important to include adaptive behavior in an assessment for higher functioning children on the autism spectrum who, despite great cognitive abilities, often have significant delays in certain areas of adaptive behavior. For example, they may lag behind in gross-motor development or may fail to achieve independence in self-help skills at typical ages.

School-Related Skills

Many skills influence success in school. A student may perform skills, but only under certain conditions. Another child may have difficulty demonstrating skills in group contexts or in novel environments. Communicative abilities may be limited for certain students, either posing difficulties in comprehending what is said to them or in the ability to articulate their own needs or concerns. Play interests may be immature, narrow, or rigid. Children may have trouble with social circumstances involving initiation, responding to others, or even understanding what is expected.

Key areas assessed in this context include (a) the ease with which the individual transfers skills across environments (generalization) and (b) core skills in multiple areas.

Generalization. Myriad skills are required in school that do not appear on tests of cognitive ability, but that are nevertheless extremely relevant for success. Perhaps the greatest issue in this regard is generalization of skills. If a student does not demonstrate skills in multiple settings, in non-treatment settings and in natural environments, acquisition of a given skill is meaningless. Furthermore, the level of independence with which the skill is performed and the degree to which it is spontaneously demonstrated are highly relevant dimensions of functioning.

The Assessment of Basic Language and Learning Skills-Revised (ABLLS; Partington & Sundberg, 1998; ABLLS-R; Partington, 2006) examines the extent to which learners possess and spontaneously demonstrate critical skills in natural environments. Highly relevant skill sequence domains include group instruction and classroom routine skills. The ABLLS (see Table 2.7) also enables precise assessment of skills, as it allows for ratings of the independence level of the skill (e.g., with or without prompts), depth of the skill (e.g., duration of task, length of group session), and breadth of the skill (including assessment of generalization of the skill). The ABLLS may also be used to select objectives to work on, and to track learner progress over time.

Table 2.7
Sample ABLLS-R Items Related to Independence

GROUP INSTRUCTION
- Sits appropriately in small group
- Sits appropriately in large group
- Attends to teacher in group
- Attends to other students in group
- Follows group instructions to all do same receptive response
- Follows group instructions with discrimination
- Raises hand to get teacher attention to do an activity
- Raises hand to answer a question
- Raises hand and names item
- Raises hand and answers a question
- Takes turns during instruction
- Learns new skills in group teaching format

CLASSROOM ROUTINE
- Follows daily routines
- Works independently (non-academic tasks)
- Sits and waits appropriately during transitions
- Physically transitions to next activity/area
- Waits turn to do activities
- Gets in line on request
- Works independently (academic activities)
- Gets and returns own materials
- Completes task and brings to teacher or puts away
- Stands and wait appropriately during transitions

The ABLLS also focuses on the development of language skills. While language acquisition is not always a major concern for higher functioning learners, the ABLLS's focus on the depth and breath of skill development and on the generalization of acquired skills makes it a relevant assessment tool for even the most able learners. The focus on how language is used is especially compelling, as many higher functioning students fail to initiate requests or interactions, to ask for help, to assert themselves, or to continue conversations. Table 2.8 lists sample items related to language use.

Table 2.8
Sample Items from ABLLS Related to Use of Language

- Spontaneously requests
- Answers novel questions
- Tells stories
- Labels emotions of others
- Labels social interaction behavior

Assessing how students use their language abilities can be challenging, and must involve capturing natural occurrences of communication. Often it is helpful to use narratives (ongoing descriptions of encounters) to identify deficits. Some teachers find it helpful to log occasions on which students require teacher assistance. A sample log is provided in Table 2.9.

Table 2.9			
Sample Language Log			
ACTIVITY	**PROBLEM**	**OUTCOME**	**IMPLICATION/GOAL**
Scooter	Grabbed scooter and hit child	Sent to bench	Teach request
			Reinforce request
Scooter	Screamed when told to wait	Calmed	Teach request
			Reinforce request
			Reinforce waiting
Scooter	Grabbed scooter	Modeled re-quest	Practice request
			Reinforce request
Bubbles	Watched others play	Prompted	Initiation training
Bubbles	Watched	Peer prompt	Initiation training
			Peer reinforcement

ANDREW'S log shows difficulties in using language appropriately. In the first instance, he grabbed a scooter from a peer and hit him in gym. The teacher sent Andrew to the bench, a form of inclusive time-out often used in that setting. In the next instance, Andrew screamed when told by the teacher to wait. In the third instance, when the gym teacher modeled how to request a turn, Andrew appropriately requested the scooter. However, the repeated nature of the problem and the fact that behaviors were escalating caused the team to discuss it at their meeting. The team realized that he needed both practice and reinforcement to build this skill.

In the next examples, Andrew simply watched a group of kids play with bubbles. When the teacher prompted him to join, he eagerly did. This was then extended to peer initiation training, so that peers would invite him to join them. The team continued to reinforce peers who made social bids to Andrew, but also developed strategies to increase his own initiation skills by practicing in other contexts, reinforcing contacts with peers, and creating rule cards and social stories to review.

Conversational skills may also pose difficulty. Being able to stay on topic, being able to shift topics with a conversational partner, and being able to end conversations are all important social navigation skills. These skills are best assessed in the natural environment. Logs and samples of conversations can shed light on where the communicative breakdowns occur, and can assist in pinpointing areas for training. Other language-related survival skills include interpreting figurative language, nonverbal communication, jokes and sarcasm, and matching the communication to the context or environment.

The student with HFA/AS may require assistance with these types of language interpretations and with understanding appropriate communication in the school environment. Helping students with ASD to comprehend communication and rules about communicating makes them more socially successful, more independent, less prone to behavioral outbursts, and less vulnerable to teasing or bullying.

Play Skills and Social Skills

Play and social skills are intertwined in the development of all young children. The way children are social with each other unfolds in play, and play itself is the context in which children make social connections. A child with poorly developed play skills or rigid play interests will struggle in making social connections and friendships, may receive fewer social bids, and may even be avoided by peers. Helping children with HFA/AS develop play skills helps to increase the likelihood of their successful social integration.

Play skills. An examination of play skills should be part of a comprehensive assessment of young children. Intervention in play skills will help to encourage skill development, increase opportunities for functional use of language, and enhance opportunities for socialization. Specifically, it is important to assess how well students can play with others, how well they can imitate peers, how reciprocal their play skills are, and how well developed their joint attention skills are. Some of these skills can be partially assessed through subsections of the ABLLS. Other assessment instruments may also help to illuminate areas of strength and deficit in these domains. Table 2.10 shows an example of a log for recording a child's free play.

Table 2.10 *Sample Free Play Log for Sam*			
ACTIVITY	**PROBLEM**	**OUTCOME**	**IMPLICATION/GOAL**
Free play (soft blocks)	Continued during blocks	Intervened-Turn taking	Tolerate others' ideas
Free play (dress-up)	Wanted to be king	Had to exit	Tolerate other roles

SAM'S log above shows several difficult moments for a child who had most difficulty during free play. Sam's major issue was that he wanted to orchestrate group activities. At times, this was fine, as peers were in agreement with his plans. However, sometimes peers had ideas of their own. Sam tended to want to repeat themes with the same activities. He wanted to build carwashes with soft blocks and to be the king during dress-up activities.

Sam's team realized these issues by logging his difficulties. They then developed goals of tolerating the ideas of peers in play activities and tolerating assignment of other roles in pretend play activities. They were able to develop analog practice sessions to build up his capacity to tolerate these alterations in his plans for play activities.

Quill (1995, 2000) offers excellent suggestions for observing and planning for play skill development, including looking at both the symbolic and the social dimensions of play (see also Wolfberg, 2003).

In the *symbolic dimension of play*, a child may exhibit no interaction with toys, manipulation of toys (which may involve gazing, mouthing, or lining up), functional use of toys (which involves the conventional use of toys and is associated with some delayed imitation), or symbolic use of toys (which involves representational play, and could involve role-playing and object substitutions). In the *social dimension of play*, an assessor can look for levels of social interest and awareness. This may range from isolated play to orientation (awareness of other children), parallel/proximity play (involving use of same space or materials as peers), and common focus (involving turn taking and active sharing of materials).

Quill, Bracken, and Fair's (2000) Assessment of Social and Communication Skills for Children with Autism breaks play behaviors into solitary and social play, and examines whether the skill is present and whether it is generalized. The depth and breadth of play skills is central in this model. This assessment also helps to operationalize exactly where a child is within a particular realm of play. For example, can he take turns, but only with one other person and only when turns are completely predictable? Can he engage in parallel play, but only when he has his own set of toys and is not required to share materials?

Table 2.11 lists categories of play behaviors commonly assessed.

Table 2.11
Categories of Play Behaviors Assessed

SOLITARY

Functional (uses one action with one toy)

Functional (close-ended activities)

Functional (open-ended activities)

Symbolic (routine scripts)

Symbolic (creative)

SOCIAL

Playing parallel with own set of materials

Playing parallel with organized materials

Participating in choral/unison group activity

Turn taking (one partner, predictable turns)

Turn taking (group, predictable turns)

Sharing materials

Cooperative play (one partner)

Cooperative play (structured groups)

Cooperative play (unstructured groups)

Wolfberg (2003) emphasizes the importance of a comprehensive assessment of play. Thus, her Play Skill Questionnaire (see Table 2.12) analyzes play experience, the diversity of play the child exhibits, the child's social play style, and developmental play patterns. This assessment can be given periodically throughout a child's educational experiences, which provides a context for assessing areas of improvement as well as those in need of continued instruction.

Table 2.12
Sample Items from Play Skill Questionnaire (Wolfberg, 1993)

PART I: PLAY EXPERIENCE

How often does child have regular opportunities to play?

Where does child regularly play?

PART II: DIVERSITY OF PLAY

Whom does child spontaneously seek out for play?

What kinds of activities does child spontaneously seek out for play? (with checklist)

Does child exhibit any of the following characteristics in play? (e.g., rituals, repetitive themes, unusual fascinations, obsessions)

PART III: PEER RELATIONS (SOCIAL PLAY STYLE)

Does child have a mutual friendship with another child?

What is child's primary mode of communication with peers?

PART IV: DEVELOPMENTAL PLAY PATTERNS

Which best describes child's social play patterns? (isolate; orientation/onlooker; parallel/proximity; common focus; common goal)

Which best describes child's representational play patterns? (manipulation/sensory; functional; symbolic/pretend; other)

Other ways to assess play skill development include the Developmental Play Assessment (DPA; Lifter, 2000; Lifter, Sulzer-Azaroff, Anderson, & Cowdery, 1993), which is designed to assess the spontaneous play behaviors of children in an effort to design appropriate skill acquisition programs.

In this semi-structured assessment of play skills, a variety of interesting and age-appropriate toys are presented to the child, and the child's play behaviors are observed and categorized. Behaviors appropriate for solitary and cooperative play are noted. There is also an emphasis on identifying emerging skills, so that intervention can strengthen skills that are beginning to be demonstrated. The DPA is made up of categories of play that represent sequential progress in the development of play behavior. The categories are listed in Table 2.13.

Table 2.13
Developmental Play Assessment – Categories of Play

LEVEL I
Indiscriminate actions (all objects treated alike)
Examples: mouths, throws, or bangs all objects

LEVEL II
Discriminative actions with single objects (differentiates & preserves conventional characteristics)
Examples: rolls beads, squeezes stuffed animals

Taking-apart combinations (separates configurations of objects)
Examples: takes apart puzzles, takes nesting cups apart

LEVEL III
Presentation combinations (recreates combinations of objects)
Examples: nests nesting cups, puts pieces into puzzle

General combinations (container/contained relations)
Examples: puts blocks in a truck, beads in a bowl

Pretend self (relates objects to self)
Examples: brings spoon to mouth, covers self with blanket

LEVEL IV
Specific combinations – physical attributes (preserves objects in configuration)
Examples: strings beads, stacks blocks

LEVEL V
Child as agent (extends familiar actions to dolls, with child as agent of activity)
Examples: extends cup to doll's mouth, puts figure in car

Specific combinations - conventional attributes (preserves unique conventional characteristics of configuration)
Examples: places cup on saucer, uses tools on car

Table 2.13 (cont.)

LEVEL VI
Single-scheme sequences (extends same action to two or more figures)
Examples: combs hair of doll and lamb, gives cup to doll and stuffed pig

Substitutions (uses one object in place of another)
Examples: puts bowl on head for hat, uses drum stick as thermometer

LEVEL VII
Doll as agent (moves doll figures as if they can move)
Examples: puts mirror in doll's hand to see itself, moves figure to load blocks into a truck

Multischeme sequences (extends different actions to same figure)
Examples: feeds doll with spoon, wipes her face and puts her to bed

LEVEL VIII
Sociodramatic play (adopts familiar roles in play theme)
Examples: plays house with varied roles; plays barbershop; plays tea party

Thematic fantasy play (adopts roles of fantasy characters)
Examples: Plays Spiderman, Power Rangers, Power Puff Girls

Social skills. Checklists also exist for examining social skills, particularly as they relate to success in the school environment. The Preschool and Kindergarten Behavior Scales (Merrell, 1994) allow teachers to rate students on a variety of items relevant to social skills and success in school. For example, the social skill section includes items such as shares toys and other belongings; accepts decisions made by adults; apologizes for accidental behavior that may upset others; compromises with peers when appropriate; and takes turns with toys and other objects. It also includes a section on problem behavior that can be used as part of a behavioral assessment, and may be followed up with a functional assessment.

Another tool, the Scales for Predicting Successful Inclusion (SPSI; Gilliam & McConnell, 1997), is designed for students beginning at age 5, so some of the items are less relevant for young learners. The instrument asks raters to evaluate students on four dimensions relevant to success in the social realm and the school environment; work habits, coping skills, peer relationships, and emotional maturity.

The ratings take the form of comparison to an average child of the same age. The focus on comparison to peers of the same age highlights the areas in which a student is very discrepant from his or her classmates. This instrument may help to identify areas of strength and of weakness, and may be helpful in prioritizing issues and skills for intervention. Table 2.14 lists sample items from the SPSI.

Table 2.14
Sample Items from the SPSI

WORK HABITS
   Following classroom rules
   Following teacher's verbal directions

COPING SKILLS
   Accepting not getting his or her own way
   Coping appropriately if someone takes something of his or hers

PEER RELATIONSHIPS
   Initiating activities with others
   Skillfully ending conversations with peers

EMOTIONAL MATURITY
   Smiling and laughing appropriately
   Expressing sympathy towards peers appropriately

Motivation

In recent years, educators have become much more sophisticated in their understanding of how to motivate students. Students with special needs often do not perform for the motivators most readily available to and preferred by typically developing learners, such as self-satisfaction and the approval of others. Instead, they require external rewards to put forth their best efforts.

This is especially true for learners with HFA/AS. In particular, when tasks are difficult or are not preferred, these learners need assistance to be motivated to learn. As a result, it is important that educators invest time and energy in identifying objects and activities that a learner will be motivated to obtain. Such information may be gathered through a variety of sources, as discussed in the following.

Indirect methods include checklists such as the Reinforcer Assessment for Individuals with Severe Disabilities (RASID; Fisher, Piazza, Bowman, & Amari, 1996) or interviews with parents and caregivers about what the child finds rewarding. The RASID asks a number of specific questions about sensory preferences, about items such as sounds, smells, and visual stimuli that the child might enjoy.

More *direct methods* of preference assessment include observing what a student is naturally drawn to and informally presenting an array of options to assess his or her interest in novel items. For example, teachers can watch how long a student engages with an object, whether she is happy while playing with an object, whether she resists giving up an object, and whether she wishes to access the object again.

The provision of a choice is in and of itself rewarding to nearly everyone. Many students react well to choosing a reward themselves. Therefore, it is important to involve students in selecting their reward, rather than the adult choosing one for them. Furthermore, having access to novel and high-interest activities helps sustain effort for difficult or non-preferred tasks. Learning will proceed more efficiently when such rewards are embedded in the task.

Occasionally, a member of the educational team may question whether students should be "rewarded" for behavior that is otherwise expected of them. Alternately, someone might raise the issue of fairness to other students. Such concerns are usually easily managed. Of course, we hope that students will do what is expected of them, but many need help getting to that level. We must start out by meeting them at their level to ensure success and progress.

There are many things we can do to increase the likelihood that students will not need the assistance of direct rewards for a long period of time. We can thin the schedule of reinforcement (i.e., provide rewards less often) methodically and in response to their success. We can also pair rewards with social praise. Eventually, we can fade out the tangible reward and simply provide praise (much as we would do for a typically developing youngster). Finally, we can link the behavior at school to rewards at home, so that the rewards are delayed until the child comes home.

With regard to fairness to other students, children generally understand the need for different types of rewards for some students. They may already know a great deal about what is difficult for a particular learner and may be able to understand the need for extra assistance in a particular area. This is especially true if the children have participated in sensitivity training to highlight compassion for differences among students. If peers are aware of areas of behaviors a student is working on, they are also more likely to understand the need for specialized incentives or rewards. (It is important to balance such information with discussions of what the student with HFA/AS does well.) It may also be possible for the teacher to create a group contingency. That is, students may all be earning rewards for goals unique to them, or the entire class could be rewarded for a similar goal.

The bottom line is that we may limit what the student is able to achieve if we fail to provide incentives. To maximize success, therefore, attention to motivation is essential. In the case illustrated below, a student is struggling with several central activities in the classroom. He has the ability to do everything that is required, but has difficulties with the social demands and with the rules of the activities. His teacher creates some incentives to help him cope with these demands and, therefore, perform at a more representative level.

ZACHARY had difficulty in a few areas. While his math skills were above those of his peers, he was struggling during math activities. Often the teacher wanted the class to work in small groups, but Zachary wanted to work alone. When he was assigned to a group, he refused to participate. Sometimes he kept the group from getting their work done, because he whined and grabbed the materials they were supposed to use.

Mrs. Walsh wasn't sure what to do, but she knew that Zachary enjoyed working alone, especially on math tasks. She created an incentive whereby Zachary could earn 10 minutes of play on math computer game if he cooperated with his group.

Zachary was also struggling in reading groups. He wanted to read each page aloud, and was impatient when other students were asked to read. Mrs. Walsh made a rule card for Zachary outlining what was expected of him in reading groups. After each page in which he followed the rules, she gave him a thumbs-up signal. At the end of the activity, if he had followed the rules, he earned a reptile (reptiles were his special interest) sticker he could put in a special book.

Figure 2.1 is an example of a rule card.

Figure 2.1. Sample rule card.

Functional Assessment

One of the major advances in understanding challenging behaviors among persons with ASD in recent years has been the use of functional assessment. Functional assessment identifies the physical and environmental factors that affect learning and behavior, and is increasingly considered to be a necessary element of effective educational service provision (Durand & Crimmins, 1987; Powers, 1997). Briefly, functional assessment involves gathering information about an individual's behavior and about the environment (O'Neill et al., 1997) for the purpose of finding functional relationships between specific behaviors and environmental variables (antecedents and consequences) that are associated with the behavior.

Behavior is functional, purposeful, and communicative. In other words, behavior is not random, but occurs for a purpose and persists because it meets a need or desire. For example, a learner may tear up a worksheet because doing so gets her out of the task (to escape a demand). Or she may pull the hair of a classmate because the teacher comes right over to her (to gain attention).

Functional assessment information may be gathered via interview, through direct observation, and through systematic manipulations (O'Neill et al., 1997).

In *interviews*, persons involved (e.g., teachers, parents) offer information about the challenging behavior via a structured format. Generally, questions cover areas such as triggers for the behavior (what seems to cause a behavior), times at which the behavior is likely and not likely to occur, environmental factors associated with the behavior, and general information about the child that may be related to behavior problems (such as sleep patterns and eating habits).

In *direct observation,* there is a focus on identifying the events that occur right before a challenging behavior (antecedents) and events that occur following a behavior (consequences). By examining many instances of a challenging behavior, patterns in antecedents and consequences can be identified.

Finally, in *systematic manipulation,* some aspect of the environment is changed to assess the impact on the challenging behavior itself; for example, a child may be given a nonpreferred task or a teacher may divert her attention to another student.

We will now look at each of these procedures in more detail.

Interviews

A number of instruments and tools are available to clinicians and educators engaging in functional assessment. Some of these instruments are checklists that team members can complete. The Motivation Assessment Scale (MAS; Durand & Crimmins, 1988) and the Functional Analysis Screening Tool (FAST; Iwata, 2002; Iwata & DeLeon, 1995) are both used for initial screenings of challenging behaviors. The MAS (discussed below) is a checklist completed by team members, while the FAST is a brief interview (that may also be filled out as a checklist). Both of these instruments are designed to be completed by several key team members who know the student well.

The Functional Assessment Interview (FAI) and Functional Assessment Observation form (O'Neill et al., 1997) are more extensive interview/observation tools that allow for more in-depth analysis of challenging behavior. All of these tools have been used extensively with many individuals with autism.

In addition, Aspy and Grossman (2007a) recently published a checklist, Underlying Characteristics Checklist (UCC), that comes in two forms, one for high-functioning (UCC-HF) and another for individuals with "classical" autism (UCC-CL). These needs assessment tools are designed to facilitate intervention design. We will briefly review a few of these tools.

The *Motivation Assessment Scale* (MAS; Durand & Crimmins, 1988) is a 16-item questionnaire that categorizes function into four categories: attention, escape, tangible items, and self-stimulation. This instrument is clear to staff and easy to administer, and it can be useful in developing hypotheses about the function of behavior. However, its utility is variable depending on the behaviors being investigated, and it may be subject to clinician bias (Duker, Sigafoos, Barron, & Coleman, 1998). For example, a teacher may believe a child is engaging in a certain behavior to gain teacher attention when, in fact, there are other important contributing factors, such as tasks that are too difficult or work sessions that are too long.

The *Functional Assessment Screening Tool* (FAST; Iwata & DeLeon, 1995) is a brief interview/checklist designed to help analyze a specific behavior and shed light on a person's general behavioral profile. It consists of 18 statements about the behavior of interest and variables that may be maintaining it. The FAST explores social reinforcement (attention, access to activities and escape) as well as automatic reinforcement (sensory stimulation, experience of pain).

The MAS, the FAST, the UCC, and other brief interview/checklist/informant measures are easy to use and quick to administer, but since they are indirect methods of functional assessment, it is recommended that such measures be used in combination with direct observations. See Table 2.15 for sample items from the MAS and the FAST.

Table 2.15
Sample Items from the FAST and the MAS

FAST

(answered as yes/no)

- The person usually complains or resists when asked to perform a task.
- The behavior occurs at high rates regardless of what is going on around the person.
- The behavior usually occurs in the presence of other persons.

MAS

(rated on a scale of 0 to 6)

- Does this behavior occur following a request to perform a difficult task?
- Does this behavior occur when you are talking to other people in the room?
- Does this behavior ever occur to get an object, activity, food, or game that the client has been told he/she can't have?

The Underlying Characteristics Checklist (Aspy & Grossman, 2007a) is an informal assessment tool designed specifically to identify characteristics across a number of domains associated with ASD for the purpose of intervention. As such, it is a component of the Ziggurat model (Aspy & Grossman, 2007b), a process for comprehensive intervention design. The UCC is comprised of seven areas of behavior: Social; Restricted Patterns of Behavior, Interests, and Activities; Communication; Sensory Differences; Cognitive Differences; Motor Differences; and Emotional Vulnerability. An eighth underlying factor is Known Medical and Other Biological Factors. The UCC may be completed individually or as a team process, including parents, teachers, or other service providers, and when appropriate, the individual who is the focus of the UCC. Table 2.16 shows the first three items under the social domain.

Table 2.16
UCC – Sample Items from Social Domain

Area	Item	✔	Notes	Follow-Up
SOCIAL	1. Has difficulty recognizing the feelings and thoughts of others (mindblindness)	✔	• *Does not recognize when classmates tease or "set her up"* • *After being corrected at home, she repetitively asks her parents if they are still angry* • *In role plays, she can accurately identify the feelings of others 4 out of 10 times*	
	2. Uses poor eye contact			
	3. Has difficulty maintaining personal space, physically intrudes on others	✔	• *Sniffs peers' hair*	

The Functional Assessment Interview (O'Neill et al., 1997) is an elaborate and in-depth interview that can be given to the individual him or herself, or to his or her parents, teachers, and other relevant individuals. Information includes specific details about the setting as well as antecedents and consequences. Additionally, a great deal of other relevant information is gathered, including details about the individual's communicative abilities, access to reinforcers, and response to previous interventions.

The interview leads to the development of hypotheses for the given behavior. Examples of hypotheses that may be generated after in-depth interview include:

• Johnny engages in spitting when faced with nonpreferred work.

• Elisa throws materials when teachers are busy.

Hypotheses can then be strengthened or refuted through direct observation. For example, someone may observe Johnny and write down all instances of spitting. In the morning work session, they note that Johnny engaged in spitting when presented with math worksheets, when asked to color a cow, and when asked to practice writing letters. On the other hand, he engaged in no spitting during sensory activities, when at gym, during play centers, or during reading group. One possibility that emerged from the observation, and that supported the hypothesis, was that Johnny disliked writing tasks.

Similarly, someone might observe Elisa, and record the instances in which she throws materials. They may note that she threw three times in an hour: When the teacher was called to the phone, when the principal came in to speak to the teacher, and when another child threw up and the teacher went to tend to her. In all three cases, reduced teacher attention appeared to be a factor, supporting the previously generated hypothesis.

Direct Observation

As mentioned, ideally, any information gathered from an interview should be corroborated with observational data. This ensures that we are observing the behavior in real circumstances and that we get real-life examples to substantiate the hypotheses. At times, someone may observe the child for a portion of the day and keep a running narrative log of all activities and behaviors. More often, direct observational information is gathered via sequential analyses, or A-B-C analyses.

Observational collection of A-B-C (antecedent-behavior-consequence) data is the standard method for gathering information about behavior and variables affecting it (Miltenberger, 1998). Such data may be gathered with a standard form or with informal forms (see Figures 2.2 and 2.3). Evaluating repetition and patterns helps to develop hypotheses regarding the function of specific challenging behaviors.

Date and Time	Setting	Antecedents	Behavior	Consequence
	☐ Outing ☐ Free Play ☐ Dinner/Lunch ☐ Bedroom ☐ Other _____	☐ Pres Demand ☐ Divert Attn ☐ Remove Attn ☐ Remove Pref ☐ Transition ☐ Other _____	☐ Aggression ☐ Screaming ☐ Disruption ☐ Noncompliance ☐ Locking Self in Bathroom ☐ Other _____	☐ Reprimand/Talk to ☐ Break from Work ☐ Ignore ☐ Work Through ☐ Other _____
	☐ Outing ☐ Free Play ☐ Dinner/Lunch ☐ Bedroom ☐ Other _____	☐ Pres Demand ☐ Divert Attn ☐ Remove Attn ☐ Remove Pref ☐ Transition ☐ Other _____	☐ Aggression ☐ Screaming ☐ Disruption ☐ Noncompliance ☐ Locking Self in Bathroom ☐ Other _____	☐ Reprimand/Talk to ☐ Break from Work ☐ Ignore ☐ Work Through ☐ Other ☐_____
	☐ Outing ☐ Free Play ☐ Dinner/Lunch ☐ Bedroom ☐ Other _____	☐ Pres Demand ☐ Divert Attn ☐ Remove Attn ☐ Remove Pref ☐ Transition ☐ Other _____	☐ Aggression ☐ Screaming ☐ Disruption ☐ Noncompliance ☐ Locking Self in Bathroom ☐ Other _____	☐ Reprimand/Talk to ☐ Break from Work ☐ Ignore ☐ Work Through ☐ Other ☐_____
	☐ Outing ☐ Free Play ☐ Dinner/Lunch ☐ Bedroom ☐ Other _____	☐ Pres Demand ☐ Divert Attn ☐ Remove Attn ☐ Remove Pref ☐ Transition ☐ Other _____	☐ Aggression ☐ Screaming ☐ Disruption ☐ Noncompliance ☐ Locking Self in Bathroom ☐ Other _____	☐ Reprimand/Talk to ☐ Break from Work ☐ Ignore ☐ Work Through ☐ Other ☐_____
	☐ Outing ☐ Free Play ☐ Dinner/Lunch ☐ Bedroom ☐ Other _____	☐ Pres Demand ☐ Divert Attn ☐ Remove Attn ☐ Remove Pref ☐ Transition ☐ Other _____	☐ Aggression ☐ Screaming ☐ Disruption ☐ Noncompliance ☐ Locking Self in Bathroom ☐ Other _____	☐ Reprimand/Talk to ☐ Break from Work ☐ Ignore ☐ Work Through ☐ Other ☐_____

ABC DATA SHEET   **DATE:** _____

Figure 2.2. Sample standard data collection form.

ABC Analysis Log						
Student's Name						
Date	Initials	Time	Setting	Antecedent	Behavior	Consequence

Figure 2.3. Sample informal data collection form. Douglass Developmental Disabilities Center, Rutgers University. Used with permission.

Sometimes interview and observation data fail to identify a clear factor relating to the presence of a behavior. At other times, information and observation identify multiple functions for a behavior. While some behaviors are genuinely multifunctional, others simply appear that way until a more thorough assessment has been completed. At these times, it may be necessary to do a functional analysis.

Functional Analysis

It may not be necessary to do a functional analysis (FA), as most behaviors are adequately assessed with a direct observational measure such as A-B-C analysis (combined with a thorough interview). Functional analysis is a more elaborate assessment protocol that is usually done by a doctoral-level psychologist and/or a certified behavior analyst. As mentioned below, it is not always possible to conduct a functional analysis in the natural environment, as it requires major alteration in activities and interactions.

Systematic experimental manipulations. In a functional analysis, staff members record what happens to the rate of a behavior when environmental variables are controlled and systematically manipulated (e.g., Carr & Durand, 1985; Iwata, Dorsey, Slifer, Bauman, & Richman, 1994; O'Neill et al., 1997). For example, if it is hypothesized that both demands and attention play a role in a behavior, staff may want to better understand how this happens. They may want to present (a) a high-demand, low-attention condition; (b) a high-demand, high attention condition; (c) a low-demand, high-attention condition; and (d) a low-demand, low-attention condition. Most functional analyses are done in clinical settings, where variables can be more readily controlled and the environment can be made maximally safe.

Simple functional analyses may be done at school, but conditions are usually briefer, as there are major logistical and safety concerns. Staff may do brief (10 minutes or less) sessions in each of these conditions several times over a few days, and then analyze the rates of the behaviors across the different conditions. This is done to find functional relationships; that is, to identify what variables lead to high rates of the behavior. It may be that demands are only a problem if attention is also low. In this case, staff can ensure availability of extra attention during stressful or difficult tasks. While there have been some recent encouraging recommendations on how to do functional analyses in school settings, many FAs are done in clinical settings. The major factor in doing functional analysis in school settings is staff training, as the expertise is specialized.

Goals of Functional Assessment

When a functional assessment/analysis is complete, the team has a good idea of why a behavior is happening, which in turn helps them to determine ways to address the behavior. The focus in treatment is on reducing the behavior, and this is primarily achieved through antecedent (preventive) strategies and through teaching replacement skills. For example, for the child who tore up worksheets to get out of a task, a variety of antecedent strategies might be used, such as fewer items on worksheets, presenting material as a matching task with manipulatives, providing higher amounts of reinforcement for difficult tasks, and interspersing paper-and-pencil activities with other activities. The student may also be helped to develop a replacement skill, or an alternative way to communicate frustration. For example, she may be given a break card (see Figure 2.4) that she can use to get a brief break from the worksheet task. More such interventions will be presented in the following chapter.

Figure 2.4. Sample break card.

Sensory Assessment

Several authors have stressed the importance of assessing the sensory issues of students with ASD (e.g., Myles et al., 2000). While there is a lack of empirical evidence about the effectiveness of sensory-based procedures, anecdotal reports of progress are plentiful, and many students on the autism spectrum receive sensory-based treatments.

A variety of sensory assessments are available that can help teams to identify and manage sensory issues. Formal assessments include The Sensory Profile (Dunn, 1999a), which also offers a shortened version, the Short Sensory Profile (Dunn, 1999b). Table 2.17 lists the major areas covered in the Sensory Profile. The short version is a 38-item form that may be used as a screening tool to determine if more in-depth assessment is needed.

Table 2.17
Sensory Profile Sample Items (from Dunn, 1999b)

SENSORY PROCESSING
Auditory processing
Responds negatively to loud or unexpected noises

Visual processing
Covers eyes or squints to protect eyes from light

Vestibular processing
Becomes anxious or distressed when feet leave the ground

Touch processing
Expresses distress during grooming

Multi-sensory processing
Has difficulty paying attention

Oral sensory processing
Mouths objects

MODULATION
Sensory processing related to endurance/tone
Has a weak grasp

Modulation related to body position/movement
Seems accident-prone

Modulation of movement affecting activity level
Prefers quiet, sedentary play

Modulation of sensory input affecting emotional responses
Rigid rituals in personal hygiene

Modulation of visual input affecting emotional responses and activity level
Avoids eye contact

Tuning into the sensory preferences of individuals with ASD can make teaching significantly more effective. For example, examining tactile preferences will help in understanding students' choice of materials, their reaction to proximity to other students, and their aversions to common activities or foods. Visual, olfactory, and auditory sensitivities may also be present. A student may have difficulty tolerating fluorescent lighting, reading text repeatedly, enduring the blare of a fire alarm, tuning out the interfering noise of heaters, or tolerating the smell of art or cleaning supplies.

Many students with such sensitivities experience behavioral difficulties in reaction to these sensations. It may be helpful to become a detective in this area, and to actively identify strategies that fit a particular child's needs. The Incident-Interpretation-Intervention approach (see Table 2.18) described by Myles et al. (2000) can be helpful in linking interventions to behaviors with a sensory function.

This approach is strengthened by the collection of data that can corroborate the effectiveness of the sensory hypotheses.

Table 2.18
Sample Incident-Interpretation-Intervention

INCIDENT	INTERPRETATION	INTERVENTION
Stares intensely at people	Has difficulty knowing what stimuli to attend to	1. Auditory/visual attending cues
	May need time to process	2. Direct instruction to shift attention
	Visual acuity poor	3. Written script on shifting attention
	Auditory comprehension problems (seek overcompensation visually)	4. Social Story™ (on how others feel when stared at)
	Visual fixation to aid concentration or prevent overload	

Adapted from *Asperger Syndrome and Sensory Issues – Practical Solutions for Making Sense of the World* (p. 74), by B. S. Myles, K. T. Cook, N. E. Miller, L. Rinner, & L. A. Robbins, 2000, Shawnee Mission, KS: Autism Asperger Publishing Company. Used with permission.

MAYA exhibited several kinds of sensory hypersensitivities. She had aversions to handling materials common in the preschool, including sand at the sand table, shaving cream during art activities, play dough, and finger paints. In fact, she often had behavioral difficulties during these times. She was also sensitive to noise, and especially had trouble during fire drills, and when the air conditioner or vacuum cleaner was on. She was fearful of these noises, and sometimes hid under her desk when she heard them. Her educational team did the incident-interpretation-intervention approach as follows.

Incident	Interpretation	Intervention
Fearful of noise	May be hypersensitive Problem: What to attend to?	Provide headphone/earplugs Issue warnings for loud noises Use soft voice Avoid AC when possible Avoid vacuum when possible
Aversions (touch)	May be uncomfortable	Use gradual exposure Reward tolerance Provide visual cues (prepare) Allow to opt out (break card) Build duration slowly Follow up with preferred task

The Incident-Interpretation-Intervention approach led to several hypotheses that had clear implications for treatment, such as avoiding loud sounds, providing headphones to muffle sound, and making available opt-out cards to allow for escape from uncomfort-

able situations. The team had also collected baseline data on the behaviors to identify when they were happening and how frequent they were over several weeks. They were then able to implement their intervention while continuing to collect data. In this way, they could clearly see how the interventions led to reduced levels of these behaviors, thereby confirming their hypotheses.

Summary

Individuals with ASD present many assessment challenges. Diagnosis itself may be an area of ambiguity, especially for those who have well-developed skills in many areas. Yet, receiving an accurate diagnosis can be crucial to the success of the learner.

Various cognitive assessments are typically used to gain an understanding of strengths and weaknesses. When using such instruments, special attention must be paid to the development of rapport and to the assessment of special aspects of testing (e.g., timed tasks) that may be difficult for individual children. Additional skill assessments include measures of adaptive behavior, descriptions of school-relevant skills, examination of the use of language in natural contexts, and the assessment of play and social skills. Further, challenging behaviors should be examined through functional assessment methods, including direct observation. Functional analysis allows for systematic manipulation of variables to further examine the relationship between behavior and environment. It is essential to assess motivation, and to provide rewards that the individual student will find truly motivating. It may also be helpful to conduct a sensory assessment to identify sensory characteristics, preferences, and triggers for an individual child.

Creating a supportive and enriching classroom setting that takes into consideration the special needs of young learners with HFA/AS is a critical underpinning of effective use of intervention strategies. No matter how well designed and empirically tested, interventions must be delivered to a child who is prepared to learn and is as comfortable as in his or her surroundings. In the next chapter, we will look at issues related to the educational setting with a particular focus on transition planning for success.

Chapter 3

EDUCATIONAL SETTING AND TRANSITION PLANNING

Transitioning is difficult for all students with ASD, and can be especially difficult for young children. Successful transitioning requires careful planning. Preparing the environment to accommodate the needs of the learner greatly increases success. In addition, it is important to attend to the needs of all parties who may require assistance and preparation, including parents, staff, peers, and the student him/herself.

There are many educational options for students with HFA/AS. Varying levels of inclusion are optimal for different learners. Matching the student to the environment is the key to success. It is also critically important to evaluate the need for supports (ancillary therapies such as speech and occupational therapy [OT], a shadow [an instructional assistant], social skills training, etc.).

The transition to kindergarten is especially important, as it creates the foundation for all future school years. It is critically important to help staff understand the behavioral characteristics of the child with HFA/AS to (a) facilitate understanding, (b) promote a proactive approach, and (c) prevent misinterpretation of the student's behaviors. Any supports that will enhance independence (visual reminders, textual cues) can be planned into the schedule and the daily routine. In some cases, classwide interventions may be used to build prosocial skills in all students and minimize a special focus on the child with ASD.

Transition to elementary school brings unique challenges as well. In some cases, multiple teachers are part of the daily educational team, increasing the need for team cohesion and role clarification, as well as preparing the student for change and varying expectations. Furthermore, the academic demands are greater, necessitating assessment of independent work capacity, adequate rate or speed of work, and cooperative learning skills. Creative use of cooperative learning groups can foster skills in all students, highlight the strengths of the student with AS or HFA, and enable the target student to make a maximal contribution to the classroom.

In any transitioning process, it is also important to attend to the needs of peers. Sensitivity training (linked to the student or not) can increase empathy and tolerance. At times, it is helpful to equip peers with strategies for being more successful in their social bids to the student with HFA/AS (e.g., wait for a response). It is also always important to highlight similarities between students and to showcase the strengths of each and every learner in the classroom.

In this chapter, we will address how to effectively transition students into educational environments. We will discuss how to help the student adapt and ways to arrange the environment to ease that adaptation. We will review the range of options that exist for transitioning young children into school environments. Different levels of inclusion will be discussed, along with the supports that make those levels of inclusion successful. In particular, we will discuss the role of the shadow, and how that individual can facilitate the participation and success of a young child with HFA/AS. We will also explore the relevance of social skills training and peer training in helping to maximize success.

Moving into Kindergarten or First Grade

Kindergarten brings many challenges for young children. While most kindergarten classrooms emphasize play and provide a balance of structured and less structured activities, similar to preschool settings, there is nevertheless a marked contrast from preschool. In particular, there are more demands for seatwork, and there is a stronger emphasis on academic skills. Furthermore, while variability in students is respected, there are increased expectations for tolerating longer lessons, for sitting for longer periods of time, for being more independent in self-help and daily living skills, and for improved behavioral control.

One of the greatest challenges for the kindergarten teacher is to understand the unique characteristics of the child. What are his or her strengths or interests? This information can be used in building rapport and in developing of an effective motivational system. What happens when the child gets overwhelmed? What works well to calm him when agitated? What steps can be taken to prevent meltdowns?

The transition to elementary school is similarly challenging. In first grade, most of the day is structured, and an academic focus is pervasive. It is essential for the teacher to understand the accommodations that the student with HFA/AS will require, such as extra time to complete assignments or visual presentations of instructions. As early as first grade, some schools require students to transition between teachers and environments. Ensuring that the student can navigate the environment and identify key educational team players will smooth the transition.

For any of these transitions, students with HFA/AS are at risk for difficulty. They often experience more difficulty with change, become easily overwhelmed when things do not go according to plan, and become very anxious. Anxiety may be triggered by environmental factors, such as noise and crowding; by the social demands of the school setting; by the challenging nature of the tasks presented; or by the need for flexibility in adapting to changes in schedules, environments, and expectations.

Preparing the Student

Transitioning a student with HFA/AS takes careful planning from the earliest stages of instruction. In preparing for entry into a novel environment, and before the student's full-time participation in that environment, students usually benefit from visits to the new classroom. Specifically, it may help for the student to experience the environment prior to the beginning of the school year. Visits to the classroom help to orient the student to the environment and provide an opportunity to meet teaching staff with fewer distractions than on the first day of school.

While encountering the actual classroom environment is ideal, a student may also meet her new teachers and other staff outside of the classroom environment. It may be more feasible for teachers to meet at the student's home or in another part of the school (especially if the classroom is not available for the summer). Any kind of initial meeting with staff will increase familiarity, which may increase the student's comfort level.

Transition to first grade may require even more planning, especially if the child has to become familiar with multiple classrooms and several teachers. Exposing the child to the teaching staff and classrooms may help to reduce anxiety, increase the child's sense of mastery, and smooth the transition when the time comes.

Many children are also helped by reading books and watching videos about going to school. If such a book or video exists that features a favorite character, such as Barney or Franklin, this can be an excellent means of conveying information and quelling fears. Other children may be helped by the creation of a book or movie specific to themselves that shows the environment and the teachers who they will be seeing regularly once in school.

Preparing the Environment

It is important to prepare a classroom that will help the student with HFA/AS transition effectively into it and function comfortably within it. Preparing the environment is an extension of the process of getting to know the characteristics of the child.

• ***Is the child distractible?***

Consider the possible sources of distraction in the classroom, including doors, windows, boards, and so on. Give thought to the placement of the student's desk; for example, will it be near the teacher to facilitate attending?

- ### *Is the child responsive to visual cues?*

Teachers might consider posting a daily schedule and providing labels for cubbies, desks, centers, and play areas. The use of individual mats or rugs may facilitate sitting in circle. It may also be helpful to post rules for the classroom, with general behavioral expectations (raise your hand, ask permission to leave the room, use an indoor voice, etc.). Teachers might also create mini-schedules that will be used to keep the student on task during independent work activities. Reminder cards can be used to cue the student to get back on track when attention has drifted, to remind students of the steps in daily activities, to help students remain calm, or to cue them to engage in critically important social behaviors. Figure 3.1 shows a sample reminder card for cleaning up. Teaching teams might consider how to present material more visually or across multiple senses to facilitate comprehension.

Figure 3.1. Sample reminder card.

- **Does the child respond well to clear incentive systems?**

Consider creating individual and/or group-oriented motivational charts for target activities (cleaning up, listening to the teacher). Most children with HFA/AS require special systems to help motivate them effectively. Their behavioral and academic performance is often enhanced by the provision of concrete indicators of progress.

TEACHERS in the Small Wonders integrated preschool/kindergarten class put stars on a clean-up chart following all clean-up activities. Every child who participates in cleaning up during the transition time earns a star for the chart, which is placed next to their name. Children who individually participate are praised, and the whole class is praised as a group (particularly when every member has contributed). In addition, each learner begins every day with two "Listening Faces." The object is to keep your listening faces throughout the day. Any child with both listening faces at the end of the day earns two treats from a treat box (e.g., small candies). If one listening face is lost (for failure to adhere to a teacher's warning to listen), the child receives only one treat at day's end. Furthermore, if the entire class keeps both listening faces, the class does a Hip Hip Hooray cheer to celebrate (this layers a group contingency and reward on top of the individual incentive).

- **Does the child have difficulty with transitions from one activity to another?**

Consider what types of classwide signals will be given for transitions, such as warnings, songs, hand signals, or environmental cues such as dimmed lights. Decide on whether and how timers might be useful to cue transitions.

Assessing How the Environment Fosters Socialization

Ideally, the classroom environment should be structured to facilitate social interaction. Table 3.1 presents a checklist that teachers can use to evaluate how well they are achieving this goal. It may also help identify placements that foster social skills, aiding teams and parents in deciding upon the optimal classroom environment.

Table 3.1
How Well Does the Classroom Structure Facilitate Social Interaction?

☐ Are all children helped in being successful with their friends? (Are they encouraged to try again if ignored?)

☐ Are interactions during play centers mostly child-directed?

☐ Do teachers provide positive feedback to children when they are playing nicely together?

☐ Does the teacher help the children by facilitating play ideas?

☐ When appropriate, do children organize the play activity? ("Let's play," "It's your turn," "Get the big red block for the roof.")

☐ Is play between children sustained? For how long?

☐ Are students encouraged to ask others to play?

☐ Are students encouraged to ask to join friends in a play activity?

☐ Are children encouraged to display work or play effort to other children?

☐ Are children encouraged to use peers as resources?

☐ Do teachers offer the least assistance necessary to facilitate interactions?

The Range of Placement Options

The variability of students with HFA/AS is substantial. It is no surprise, therefore, that their needs are best met in a variety of settings. Matching children to their optimal learning environment is a complex endeavor that requires careful assessment and the participation of all members of the educational team.

There are major advantages to students with HFA/AS being in a mainstream, typical educational environment. For example, this is often the best environment for maximizing academic potential, for exposing students to good role models, and for maintaining their interest by keeping them intellectually stimulated.

Full inclusion with supports. Although the fully included environment may be the best option for a given child, most children with HFA/AS need specific supports to be successful in that environment. For example, the student may be at or near age level in many areas and can learn new material in a variety of natural ways, but still requires help to attend, to follow group instructions, or to complete work. The law is very clear that children have a right to be in the least restrictive environment. Supports that allow for success in the least restrictive environment should be offered.

Be reluctant to move students to a special education placement, when they could succeed in regular education. Often, a shadow may be designated to help the student to respond to the classroom teacher and to participate meaningfully in classroom activities.

CHANDRA is a high-functioning child with autism who did very well in a specialized preschool program for two years. She then spent a year attending preschool with a shadow two days a week, participating part time in special education placement. She is now entering kindergarten. While she has many academic strengths, she has a lot of difficulty socially. For example, she knocks over the block structures that her classmates create, she tends to be overly excited in her interactions with them, and her play skills are generally immature. She also has trouble with transitions. She requires frequent feedback and support, especially in circle time, and her endurance for work is shorter than that of her peers. A shadow will help ensure that Chandra receives prompts and reinforcement to maximize her participation.

Shadowing: Support Within Full Inclusion

What is a shadow? A shadow is an individual who uses systematic prompting (i.e., assistance to facilitate correct responding; Cooper, Heron, & Heward, 1987, 2007) and reinforcement (i.e., rewards delivered contingent on appropriate behavior; Cooper et al., 1987) to support a student's participation in a more inclusive, less restrictive environment.

A shadow is not a second teacher. A shadow's role is to facilitate the student's response to the classroom teacher. In essence, the shadow orients and assists the student in participating in the classroom. The goal is not to get the student to respond to the shadow. Instead, the shadow aims to get the student to respond to the classroom teacher and to peers.

How is this different from an aide? The terms *shadow, instructional aide,* or *teaching assistant* are sometimes used interchangeably to describe support in the classroom for the student with ASD.

However, it is helpful to conceptualize shadowing as distinct from instructional assistance. Some students with ASD need continuous assistance from a designated aide throughout the day. The aide may provide instruction in completely different ways from the classroom teacher, and may even teach activities that are unrelated to those going on in the classroom. However, most students with HFA/AS who need specialized help to succeed in general education do not require intrusive or continuous assistance. For example, a student may need help only when agitated or in a behavioral escalation, or only during transition times. Another student may need support to stay on task to ensure that she does not fall behind their peers as they become distracted.

A shadow supports the student with HFA/AS in responding to the natural demands in the environment, including responding to the classroom teacher. Table 3.2 outlines the major differences between the role of aide vs. shadow.

Who makes a good shadow? Many different kinds of people can serve as shadows. A unique option arises when a person who has taught the student in a home-based program or a previous educational environment expresses an interest in shadowing the student. While this can be helpful, it can also be problematic. On the positive side, a shadow who has worked with the student previously will likely have a good relationship with the student. Therefore, the child may be more responsive than he or she would otherwise be in a novel environment with many new challenges. This is a substantial advantage for learners who are likely to struggle with the transition to a new environment. A shadow with a previous history would also know the student's levels in a variety of areas, thereby streamlining the process of assessment for the teacher. Maybe most important, such an individual may know what kinds of social, tangible, and edible stimuli have served as effective reinforcers over time, ensuring that the child will be effectively motivated. The shadow may also know about specific idiosyncratic responses to various strategies. For example, he or she may know that picture cues work well, or that Social Stories™ (Gray, 1993) have successfully addressed situations involving fear. Finally, shadows who know the family may be able to suggest ways to convey or share information that would be most comfortable to the family.

Table 3.2 *Aide vs. Shadow*	
THE 1:1 AIDE	**THE SHADOW**
Devotes full attention and time to the student	Offers assistance and fosters independence
May provide special lesson or adaptations	Usually supports student in typical classroom activities
Often sits in front of or adjacent to student	Sits or stands behind student or watches from across room
Offers intrusive assistance	Offers least intrusive assistance
Offers direct reinforcement	Uses subtle forms of reinforcement whenever possible
Uses continuous or very frequent reinforcement	Reinforces periodically, and seeks to reduce reinforcement
Emphasizes skill acquisition	Emphasizes incidental learning and transfer of skills across settings
May provide modeling of desired responses	Directs student's attention to peer models
Student takes instruction from aide	Student takes instruction from the teacher
Data collection on skill acquisition	Data collection efforts typically involve the maintenance and generalization of skills, the spontaneous use of language, social interaction, etc.

Nevertheless, there are some disadvantages to a previous relationship, too. Specifically, the student may depend too much on the shadow, and familiarity may prevent or delay adaptation to new instructors. The shadow's previous relationship with the family can also present challenges. Parents may naturally direct questions and correspondence to the shadow, whom they already know, rather than to a new and unfamiliar teacher. Shadows can also sometimes inadvertently undermine the teacher's authority or breach confidentiality, while trying to be appropriate and navigate a complicated role.

How do shadows spend their time? The most critical responsibility of the shadow is to be a good observer. This is especially critical in the first few months of shadowing, during the transition to the classroom environment. Shadows assisting students with HFA/AS must attend to a wide variety of behaviors and skills (e.g., Doyle, 1997; Twachtman-Cullen, 2000). They need to watch how a student does in each segment of the day, in social situations, and during less structured times of day. The checklist in Table 3.3 gives a sample of some of the times of day that a shadow would observe to note strengths and deficits.

Table 3.3

Checklist for an Effective Shadow

WHILE THE STUDENT IS IN CLASS, THE SHADOW ENSURES THAT THE CHILD:

- ☐ Transitions to classroom appropriately (e.g., removes jacket, puts away possessions)
- ☐ Greets peers
- ☐ Sits in group appropriately and for sustained duration
- ☐ Refrains from disruptive behavior in group activities
- ☐ Raises hand at appropriate times and at a rate commensurate with his experience and knowledge
- ☐ Responds to group instruction
- ☐ Attends to teacher directions
- ☐ Initiates independent work activity when directed by the teacher without verbal protest
- ☐ Maintains himself in an independent work activity when directed by the teacher
- ☐ Maintains himself in an independent play activity when directed by the teacher
- ☐ Transitions from one class activity to the next quickly and without disruptive behavior
- ☐ Follows the rules for learning centers
- ☐ Participates in activities within learning centers
- ☐ Lines up appropriately with class
- ☐ Works quietly during quiet time
- ☐ Transitions from preferred activity to less preferred activity quickly and without disruptive behavior
- ☐ Responds to peers' initiations
- ☐ Initiates with peers in recreational activities
- ☐ Initiates with peers in group work activities
- ☐ Responds to peers in group work activities
- ☐ Eats appropriately during lunch and snack time
- ☐ Refrains from engaging in maladaptive or otherwise disruptive behaviors

Within all of these activities, there are times when the shadow needs to intervene to redirect the student's attention, to facilitate responding, or to assist in a social interaction. A wide variety of strategies can be used by a shadow to ensure success on the learner's part (e.g., Doyle, 1997; Twachtman-Cullen, 2000). One of the paramount goals of a shadow is to provide such support in ways that promote independence and reduce the likelihood of stigmatization, as outlined in Table 3.4.

Table 3.4
Goals of Shadow's Support of Child

IN THEIR INTERACTIONS WITH THE STUDENT, SHADOWS TRY TO:

1. Offer guidance and feedback in subtle, nondisruptive ways

2. Provide feedback in ways that reduce dependency

3. Promote transfer of skills to class

4. Promote the learning of new skills within the classroom

5. Constantly assess and evaluate the effectiveness of potential reinforcers

6. Enhance the student's socialization with peers

7. Facilitate learning from peers

8. Promote transitions across activities

9. Strengthen independence

10. Minimize and prevent challenging behaviors

How does a shadow accomplish these goals? In a moment, we will examine each of these goals in greater detail to specify how a shadow might facilitate a learner's performance in a classroom. Before we do, however, let's look at some of the tools that will be relied upon the most to accomplish these goals.

A wide variety of tools are nearly universally used with individuals on the autism spectrum. The tools are useful in socially complex environments in which reinforcement and attention are generally less available. Each of these will be reviewed in some detail elsewhere, but it may help to think of them as you consider the main tasks of a shadow.

Classroom Organizational Structure

Most students are helped enormously by pictorial and/or textual individualized labels of their cubbies, desks, circle spots. Furthermore, they navigate classrooms more effectively when areas are clearly labeled and cues are readily available (pictures of blocks on block shelf, etc.).

Visual Schedules

Most students respond very well to visual schedules, which indicate the order of activities for the day. Many students also benefit from mini-schedules for certain periods (e.g., play centers will consist of blocks, sensory, and dress-up). Similarly, they may benefit from step-by-step instructions for multistep activities (e.g., color the apples, cut out apples, glue apples on the apple tree).

Incentive Systems

In general, students with HFA/AS require additional motivation to achieve maximal success. While many of them respond well to group contingencies that target the behavior of all students in the room, some will require a more individualized approach. It is often helpful to present such rewards in a visual way, such as via a token system. Such incentives may be needed for sustaining attention, for tolerating group instruction, and/or for completing work. It is very helpful for students with HFA/AS to be provided with concrete and tangible rewards.

Social Stories™

Social Stories™, originated by Carol Gray (1993, 1994) and used extensively with children on the spectrum, help students understand social information. They are often used to teach children what to expect in a given situation, especially if it is a situation that often presents difficulties (e.g., playing on the playground). They can also be used as part of a package of interventions to address challenging behaviors.

Rule Cards

Rule cards come in a variety of formats and by a variety of names. They are used to help students follow rules in certain contexts. They are often used in combination with other approaches, including practicing a given behavior in analog situations. (Figure 3.1 showed a sample reminder/rule card.)

Effective Shadowing

The list above provides only a brief overview of some of the tools a shadow might rely on. The following section outlines ways in which an effective shadow accomplishes the goals of his/her role.

1. **Provides guidance and feedback in subtle, nondisruptive ways and in ways that reduce dependency**

   It is important that the shadow does not interfere in the environment, usurp the primary role of the teacher, or create dependency in the student. To prevent any of these occurrences, the teacher must ensure that primary instruction and directions come from the classroom teacher. The shadow works to help the student attend to and follow through with the teacher's instructions. The shadow recognizes that the key to success in this context is to provide the least intrusive prompt that can lead to the desired response (e.g., MacDuff,

Krantz, & McClannahan, 2001; Maurice, Green, & Luce, 1996; Snell & Brown, 2000).

One way to foster attention to the teacher is to use sight words, pictures, and photos as mechanisms for providing subtle feedback to the student. Often shadows develop a repertoire of gestures that can be used to provide the student with reinforcement or redirection. For example, they may flash the student a thumbs-up sign from a distance, rather than coming over to tell the student she has done well.

When a student needs help, a shadow offers the least intrusive assistance possible. Intrusive prompts such as physical prompts or extended verbal prompting can be disruptive and stigmatizing. Instead shadows try to offer as little assistance as possible and, when offered, assistance is brief and does not disrupt the ongoing activity. Shadows also prompt from behind or speak to the student from the side, whenever possible, to avoid becoming a central focus of attention. Shadows may wait before offering assistance (utilizing a time-delay procedure), to give the child an opportunity to respond on his own. Thus, a shadow seeks to be as minimally involved as feasible. In this way, the student is also afforded every opportunity for independence.

2. **Promotes the transfer of skills**
   One of the ways in which shadows can assist in this goal is to be aware of the need to communicate information to the teacher about skills the student possesses. This helps the teacher to include the student by calling on her to demonstrate her knowledge. When a student is somewhat reticent or reluctant to participate, the shadow can promote hand raising and responsiveness to teacher inquiries.

If a student has difficulty comprehending novel language and is unsure of what the teacher means, shadows can maintain a running log of instructions and directives that are commonly used by the teacher. In this way, parents and other team members can work to build the student's responsiveness to novel instructions. While the student is still acquiring this familiarity, shadows can translate the unfamiliar instructions to known language.

3. **Promotes the learning of new skills within the classroom**
   Shadows must also work to ensure that the student learns new skills within the classroom environment. In some ways, this is the most critical issue related to the effectiveness of the student's placement. The child must be able to acquire information within the natural lessons and interactions within the regular education setting. A child who struggles in this area may need more intensive instruction or remedial assistance.

4. **Evaluates the effectiveness of potential reinforcers**
   While motivation impacts upon every aspect of performance and participation, the role of motivation becomes even more critical when tasks are difficult, challenging, or non-preferred. A shadow can do a great deal to prevent performance problems by offering rewards that motivate the student (Snell & Brown, 2000).

One major challenge in working with students with HFA/AS is that it is not always possible to know which rewards will be effective in building compliance and performance. Shadows can do some detective work to explore which rewards are of particular interest to a child. This may be done by exposing the student to an array of novel items and watching for his or her reactions.

- Which objects does the child approach?

- Which objects does the child play with for substantial periods of time?

- Which objects are hard for the student to give up?

- Which objects appear to be preferred by the students?

5. **Enhances the student's socialization with classroom peers**

   Students with HFA/AS need help to make the most of the social environment they find themselves in. Consequently, it is important for the shadow to seek opportunities to facilitate socialization with peers during group activities.

   Some of this can be accomplished by requiring students to ask one another for assistance with tasks (such as opening juice boxes or pudding containers). Such strategies can be applied across students to prevent stigmatizing the student with ASD.

   It may also be helpful to build skills such as consistently greeting peers by creating routines around such a skill (e.g., as soon as student enters class) or by selecting a few peers to practice with on a daily basis (such as students sitting in the same group of desks or students whose cubbies/lockers are adjacent to the student).

6. **Facilitates learning from peers**

   A major strategy to assist the student in learning from peers is to focus on imitation. The shadow can encourage the child with ASD to follow the lead of classmates in a variety of tasks. Shadows can direct the student to watch peers, especially for information about what to do. For example, a shadow can instruct a student to watch her friends or a particular classmate when having to do a transition (e.g., lining up, cleaning up), when completing an independent work activity (e.g., a worksheet), or during group activities (e.g., circle time). Helping students with HFA/AS to use peers as a source of information is a survival skill. When a teacher's instruction is missed or forgotten, looking to one's classmates for information on what is expected can help the student be successful without adult intervention.

7. **Promotes transitions across activities with minimal disruptive behaviors**
Shadows accomplish this important goal by carefully planning for transitions. Shadows help the student anticipate when a transition will be occurring, providing clear cues about the length of time left in an activity. Auditory and visual timers can assist in this process.

MIGUEL struggled with transition from recess to classroom work time. This was particularly stigmatizing, because he became very agitated when the transition occurred. At times, when teachers approached him to assist him in the transition, he became aggressive. The teaching staff tried a variety of strategies to assist Miguel. They wrote a Social Story™ about following the schedule, they practiced and rehearsed effective transitioning, they videotaped peers transitioning effectively (to expose Miguel to appropriate models in a salient way), they provided warnings about the impending transition, they helped him set his watch with beeps warning of the transition's approach, and they used a visual timer during recess to help Miguel track the progress of time.

8. **Strengthens independent activities**

   Children with HFA/AS need help to be as independent as possible. They are vulnerable to becoming dependent on various types of assistance or rigid about the types of help offered to them, so every effort must be made to prevent dependency and rigidity. One strategy that helps foster independence and prevent rigidity is to use a wide variety of prompts, rather than assisting the student in the same way each time. Altering the kinds of help given may make learners more flexible, and prepares them better for natural environments. Thus, students will be better prepared to benefit from the assistance of future educators involved with them if they are exposed to a variety of prompts.

   Many of the strategies discussed here are designed to reduce prompt dependency. Strategies such as coming in and out quickly to assist as needed (as opposed to remaining next to the student at all times), providing feedback in a non-intrusive manner, and interacting with other students all help to foster independence in the target student.

9. **Minimizes and prevents challenging behaviors**

   Shadows are in an excellent position to minimize and prevent challenging student behaviors. They can anticipate which circumstances will be difficult for the child, and can prepare to minimize the difficulty. For example, a child with HFA or AS may have difficulty with change in routine, such as early dismissal, a group assembly in the auditorium, or a class picnic. A shadow can help by creating a visual schedule of the day. In this way, the student can visually reference how the day is different from other days, and can better anticipate when things will happen.

The use of Power Cards (Gagnon, 2001) can help to define critical expectations for a difficult activity, using the child's special interests as an embedded reward. Briefly, a Power Card is a portable index-sized card with a graphic and three to five points based upon a simple story written from the perspective of the child's special interest.

Some young students with HFA/AS have well-developed reading skills, so they may benefit from simple text. For many other young learners, it is better to present the information with photos of themselves engaged in the appropriate activity or with other picture-based cues. In any case, it might end with a very motivating statement (possibly paired with a picture), unique to that child.

A sample Power Card using the Sponge Bob character appears below. This particular card was used to help a young child pay attention in preschool. Copyright law prevents us from including pictures of Sponge Bob and his friends here. However, use of graphics is important, especially for young learners.

Power Card

Sponge Bob Square Pants loves to work at the Krusty Krab, but sometimes it is hard to pay attention to Mr. Krabs. At the end of a long day of making Krabby Patties, Sponge Bob is very tired and thinks it is too hard to pay attention to what Mr. Krabs tells him. But Squidward taught Sponge Bob that it is important to look, watch, listen, and answer Mr. Krabs, so he knows how to do a good job at work.

Just like Sponge Bob, it is important for kids in school to pay attention to their teachers so they know what to do. It makes Sponge Bob and his friends proud when kids remember to: Look, Watch, Listen, and Answer their teachers to do a good job in school.

A shadow provides increased reinforcement during periods of increased demands. Perhaps a student with HFA or AS needs twice as much feedback during reading than he does during math. An effective shadow will deliver feedback on different schedules during different activities to match those needs.

At times, a shadow may take descriptive data for a functional assessment of a challenging behavior or even participate in a functional analysis under the direction of the teacher or a behavior analyst, to help the team determine what the function of a given behavior is. It may be that the student is disruptive because the task is too hard or because she is seeking individual attention during a group activity. Such data can be important in guiding the development of an effective treatment plan. Behavior plans must match the function of the behavior, or they will not be effective. (For example, if a student is engaging in disruptive behavior because the work is too hard, a variety of curricular adjustments can be made. In addition, the student can be helped to express his frustration in more acceptable ways, such as asking for help or requesting a break.) Shadows will also need to take ongoing data for behavioral intervention plans, which can then be analyzed to assess the impact of the plan and the need for revisions or adjustments.

How Does a Shadow Work with the Classroom Teacher Most Effectively?

Role definition is critically important. Under the direction of the teacher, shadows and teachers agree on who is responsible for each of the specific daily tasks that must be accomplished. For example, teachers and shadows need to agree on who will write the daily note home, who will summarize the data, and who will provide regular updates to the parents on the child's progress. While the teacher remains responsible for all the child's instruction, she may wish the shadow to assume one or more of those responsibilities.

Is It Possible to Fade a Shadow's Assistance?

The role of shadows, by nature, is designed to be faded. A child who requires ongoing support over many years is in need of an instructional assistant or aide. By contrast, a child who simply needs support to participate, but who can learn in the general education environment, is in need of a shadow.

The need for shadows often declines over time. The child may need the most support in the first few years of school. Some children eventually require such support only for the first part of new school years. Other students can share the support with other students, no longer requiring a designated shadow.

There are several ways to assess readiness for fading. One way is to collect data on how and when assistance is needed. A log of the shadow's involvement can be helpful in this process. Such a log may be formatted as shown in Figure 3.3.

Shadow:_____		
Student:_____		
Date:_____		
When did I need to intervene? (activity)	**What type of help was offered? (prompts, type, & #)**	**How did the student respond?**

Figure 3.3. Log of shadow involvement.

As illustrated, the log provides information about the kinds of activities that the child is struggling with, which can assist the team in targeting certain activities or times of day. It also provides information on the kinds of assistance offered to the student. For example, it may be particularly helpful to track the number of times a shadow had to assist a learner in a given activity, as it provides an index of independence for that portion of the day.

Completed Log		
Shadow: _____Jodie_____		
Student: _____Patrick_____		
Date: _____11/17/06_____		
When did I need to intervene? (activity)	**What type of help was offered? (prompts, type, & #)**	**How did the student respond?**
Unpacking backpack	2 verbal reminders 1 gestural reminder 1 physical prompt	Ignored Ignored Worked
Sitting like a pretzel at circle	Picture cue	Worked
Sitting like a pretzel at circle	Look at your friends	Worked
Raising hand	Picture cue Tap on elbow	Did not work Worked
Cleaning up at end of play	Look at your friends	Worked
Lining up for recess	Picture cue	Worked
Listening to teacher at group	Eyes on teacher card	Worked
Getting lunchbox	Look at your friends	Worked
Answering peer	Ask friend to repeat	Worked
Soft blocks	Redirected to take turns	Agitated
Kept trying to alter	Read rule card	Still upset
What kids were building	Reminded of tokens	Still upset
	Allowed opt-out (break)	Walked to office Got water Waited for turn

Figure 3.3. Log of shadow involvement (cont.).

Training the Shadow

Shadowing requires broad-scale training. First, shadows (and all the educational professionals working with the target student) need to know about ASD and, specifically, the learning characteristics of individual students. Further, they need to know about the application of effective prompting and reinforcement procedures. They also need to be trained as astute observers and reliable data gatherers. Finally, they need to understand their role definition, and be coached in how to work effectively and productively with all members of the educational team (e.g., Cavallaro & Haney, 1999).

Most important, they need to get to know the learner to whom they have been assigned, to develop rapport, and to understand which approaches will be most successful with this learner. It may be that the child responds well to Social Stories™, to rule cards, to token systems, or to special cueing for upcoming transitions. It is essential that shadows be trained to effectively implement whatever procedures are appropriate.

Such training should include extensive modeling; comprehensive, repetitive, and ongoing feedback; and competency-based assessment of skill possession. The training literature is clear that workshops alone do not prepare staff to effectively implement procedures (e.g., McClannahan & Krantz, 1993; Noell, Witt, LaFleur, Mortenson, Ranier, & LeVelle, 2000). Staff members need to be helped to understand how to DO the approaches, with observation (modeling), rehearsal, and feedback on their performance (e.g., Alavosius & Sulzer-Azaroff, 1986; Ducharme & Feldman, 1992; Schepis, Reid, Ownbey, & Parsons, 2001; Selinske, Greer, & Lodhi, 1991).

It is complicated to arrange for such training, given that individuals who will serve in those roles may not even be hired or selected before the school year begins! All members of the team might be provided with specialized training on ASD, with a special focus on the characteristics of students with HFA/AS. Some districts might also be able to arrange for shadow training. Most important, there must be guidance for the shadow and teacher once the student arrives. A behavior analyst, school psychologist, learning consultant, special education teacher, or other knowledgeable team member may be able to provide suggestions, modeling, and feedback during the early days of instruction. They may also be able to assist in creating materials and supports that reduce the student's anxiety, such as daily schedules, rule cards, Power Cards, and motivational systems.

What Other Environmental and Teaching Supports Might Be Useful?

Other supports might also help a student to succeed in an inclusive environment. Speech therapy may be especially helpful. Many students with HFA/AS do not exhibit language delays (in reference to age norms), but may demonstrate difficulties in their use of language.

JOSHUA was at or above age level on all standardized speech evaluations. Nevertheless, effective communication remained a challenge for him. He tended not to initiate to others about his needs, but passively awaited assistance from teachers. He also rarely spontaneously requested anything he needed, passively waiting for access to the item or to be noticed by a helpful teacher or peer. In addition, while he could reply to greetings very effectively, he did not do it in a timely way. It sometimes took him 7 to 10 seconds to respond to a peer's greeting or question.

Usually, the peer had disappeared by the time Josh answered. In the same way, he was slow to respond to a teacher in a group instructional context. Often, the lag time in his responses forced the teacher to move on (for fear of losing the interest and momentum of the entire group). For these reasons, Josh missed many opportunities for social interaction and group participation. Further, some of his classmates interpreted his lack of response as disinterest in them or as incapability on his part. Finally, Josh had trouble expressing himself when he was upset. In the heat of the moment, he would simply tantrum without words, apparently unable to express his emotions verbally.

Speech therapy may help to address these targeted deficits. Intervention focused in the practical use of language can greatly increase Joshua's social and academic success.

Many students benefit from the involvement of a special educator. For example, special and general educators may co-teach in an included classroom. In this way, the special educator's expertise is made available, but the student does not lose access to the typical environment. It may be that the special educator will help the student with decoding problems in reading or with sequencing in math or with letter formation in writing.

LEAH was in first grade, but still had a lot of difficulty with pre-academic skills. In particular, her reading readiness skills were weak. She could identify some upper-case letters, but none of the ones that were similar to each other or common sources of confusion (e.g., B, P, D). She could not identify any lower-case letters except for x. She did not seem to understand the connection between letters and the sounds they make. While she could write her name correctly at times, she often wrote it right to left, and usually reversed the L and the E. There were some perceptual difficulties with numbers as well. She could not seem to comprehend how to identify numbers above 10, and she reversed 6 and 9. Her special education teacher focused on phonics and rhyming activities, exposed her to letters (especially lower case), and worked on building a left-to-right sequencing progression across multiple activities. She also integrated preferred activities into the lessons (e.g., music and art) to reduce Leah's frustration.

Social Skills: An Elusive Target

Most students with HFA/AS have difficulty with social skills, and may benefit from targeted intervention in this area (e.g., Baker, 2002, 2003; Wagner, 1999). Social skills can be addressed in a wide variety of ways, including individual instruction, group instruction, and classwide approaches.

Individually oriented instruction. It is difficult to teach social skills outside of a social context. Besides, it is less likely that interventions done outside of social situations will effect change in the natural environment. Ideally, therefore, social skills must be targeted in the natural contexts and with peers.

However, in certain circumstances social skills may be first worked on individually and then transferred to peers. For example, it may be easier for an instructor to initially work individually with a child on losing a game gracefully. The instructor would have considerably more control over the variables, and be able to manage behavioral escalations more easily. Furthermore, the child would not suffer negative social consequences with peers.

Group instruction. In some cases, a grade level or school may have several students in need of help with social skills. If so, a social skills group may be established. This can be an excellent forum from addressing many social problems. Sample goals for a social skills group are listed in Table 3.5.

Table 3.5
Sample Goals for Social Skills Group

ASKING TO JOIN IN AN ACTIVITY
- Effective strategies
- Dealing with rejection

TAKING CONVERSATIONAL TURNS
- Understanding when someone else has completed his or her turn

FOLLOWING UP IN CONVERSATION
- Keeping an interaction going
- Asking questions
- Responding to comments
- Offering similar information
- Building the number of exchanges

LEARNING NOT TO INTERRUPT
- Defining interruption
- Refraining from interruption

ASKING FOR A DESIRED TOY THAT ANOTHER STUDENT HAS
- Appropriate requesting
- Compromise

USING WORDS TO EXPRESS ANGER
- Finding the right words
- Expressing the words appropriately
- Sample scenarios and rehearsal

UNDERSTANDING THE COMMUNICATIONS OF CONVERSATIONAL PARTNERS
- Comprehending readiness to interact
- Comprehending when a partner wants to end an interaction

WINNING AND LOSING GRACEFULLY
- Controlling feelings of disappointment
- Being a good loser (e.g., finding words to congratulate the winner)

Classwide contingencies. It may be helpful for all members of a classroom to have social skills targeted within the curriculum. Classrooms might implement social teams as part of learning center activities, where students practice social skills. Teachers might also institute reward programs for all students focused on a particular social skill. For example, students might earn pennies by being nice to their friends (defined as offering help or sharing).

How are social skills taught? As discussed in detail in Chapter 4, social skills are taught in a variety of ways. Common approaches include Social Stories™ (Gray, 1993, 1994), rule cards, role-play activities, behavioral rehearsal, and video modeling. All of these strategies have major implications for success in transitioning to and in functioning within an inclusive environment. (See Chapter 4 for a thorough discussion of each strategy's applications and relevance.)

Regardless of how social skills are taught, motivation is a prime consideration. As always when working with children on the autism spectrum, concrete and visual tools, combined with the child's special interest, work the best. Figure 3.4 illustrates a self-monitoring checklist that includes the child's special interest, airplanes.

DID I ...	
	Total Points
1. Talk to a friend? (5 points) Talk to an adult? (2 points)	
2. Look at their eyes while I spoke? Yes = 2 points; No = -1 point	
3. Stand just right, facing them? Yes = 2 points; No = -1 point	
4. Listen to what they said? Yes = 2 points; No = -1 point	
5. Say something back? Yes = 2 points; No = 0 points	
TOTAL SCORE =	
1. Talk to a friend? (5 points) Talk to an adult? (2 points)	
2. Look at their eyes while I spoke? Yes = 2 points; No = -1 point	
3. Stand just right, facing them? Yes = 2 points; No = -1 point	
4. Listen to what they said? Yes = 2 points; No = -1 point	
5. Say something back? Yes = 2 points; No = 0 points	
TOTAL SCORE =	
1. Talk to a friend? (5 points) Talk to an adult? (2 points)	
2. Look at their eyes while I spoke? Yes = 2 points; No = -1 point	
3. Stand just right, facing them? Yes = 2 points; No = -1 point	
4. Listen to what they said? Yes = 2 points; No = -1 point	
5. Say something back? Yes = 2 points; No = 0 points	
TOTAL SCORE =	

Figure 3.4. Self-monitoring system using child's special interest.

Planning for Inclusion

It is critical that the instructional team decide who will coordinate the inclusion effort. Teachers, supervisors, psychologists, or other team members can all serve successfully in this role, but someone must be designated. This is especially true of the elementary school transition, where the number of players is larger. Inclusion is a major and complex undertaking, and collaboration of many professionals is the key to success (Snell & Janney, 2000). All involved team members must be aware of their responsibilities and have a forum in which they can discuss their expectations and concerns. Teachers should become familiar with inclusion strategies and behavior management strategies before the student enters the classroom (e.g., Demchak & Drinkwater, 1992; Harris & Handleman, 1997).

In addition to initial planning sessions, there should be opportunities for the team to meet together. Such training and planning is not a one-time event. Regular meetings to review the student's successes and struggles can reduce the isolation felt by individual team members in their roles and can ensure that problems are addressed in a timely fashion.

Preparing Peers

Peers are another group of consumers of the inclusive experience. There is tremendous variability in what peers can or should be told about a student with HFA/AS. Again, the variability of students makes for tremendous diversity in terms of what is appropriate to share. Parents of the child with HFA/AS may have opinions about what information they would like to have shared with classmates and how it should be shared. Therefore, they need to be key players in the decision about whether and how to prepare peers.

Sensitivity training is an excellent means of impacting more broadly the students' understanding and tolerance of difference. Such training can be very broad, generally focusing on ways in which all people are different from one another. Some schools have had success in using the Kids on the Block puppet show, which describes many disabilities, including autism, and health problems, such as asthma. Teachers might also read books about differences, and conduct simulation exercises to enhance empathy for people with disabilities. (For example, they may have students try to hear directions while wearing headphones or button up a coat while wearing mittens.)

If desired, a teacher may specifically target learning differences. For example, students may be asked to follow directions delivered too rapidly to be processed or to read a passage using backwards letters. Such activities can give students an increased capacity to understand the challenges and frustrations faced by a person with a disability.

The emphasis on differences is essential in sensitizing peers, in building empathy, and in fostering understanding. However, sometimes there is so much emphasis on the differences between children with ASD and their peers that we forget to point out the countless similarities. It is helpful to share information on how similar the child with HFA/AS is to his or her peers. For example, the child may have a dog, like to play with trains, play baseball, or take karate lessons. A parent of a child may volunteer to come tell the group about his or her child's specific characteristics or about autism in general. Parents are often in the best position to paint a true and comprehensive picture of the child, including likes, dislikes, family constellation, and interests. This information (and the focus on the whole child and how the child may be just like his friends in many ways) can help to build bridges between children.

Finally, it is important for peers to recognize that the child with HFA/AS has many strengths as well as deficits. Many students with HFA/AS perform better than their age peers in multiple areas, but peers may not automatically recognize this. They may see them as students who do not always listen, who only answer questions sometimes, or who sometimes get very upset. They will have a more accurate view of their friend if they also know what the child is good at.

To that end, teachers can look for opportunities to showcase the strong abilities of students with HFA/AS. They may be asked to read a book to the class, to solve math problems at the board, to tell the class about the solar system, or to bring in a puzzle they can do for show and tell.

Numerous resources can assist teachers in facilitating understanding among peers. Even if peers will not need training in how to interact with or assist a child with HFA/AS, it still might be helpful to do some sensitivity training for the entire classroom. In this context, it is usually a good idea to focus on identifying feelings and on things that make each person in the classroom feel differently. Teachers can extend this training into discussions of how to help friends who are experiencing difficult emotions. Some sensitivity and tolerance training for differences also facilitates understanding of specific disabilities or challenges. Autism can be one of these disorders reviewed, but others can be covered as well.

The following resources are helpful for facilitating understanding among peers and also for preparing the child with ASD him/herself for effective class participation.

Feelings

Cardon, T. (2004). *Let's talk emotions: Helping children with social cognitive deficits, including AS, HFA, and NVLD, learn to understand and express empathy and emotions.* Shawnee Mission, KS: Autism Asperger Publishing Company.
Through the activities in this book, children learn to identify and respond to their own feelings as well as the feelings of others. This improves their ability to self-regulate their emotions while also increasing their chances for more meaningful social interactions with others.

Parr, T. (2002). *The feel good book.* Boston: Little, Brown, and Company.
This book has wonderful illustrations and examples of experiences children will relate to that feel good (e.g. catching snowflakes on your tongue, sharing treats with a friend, having a ladybug land on your hand.

Parr, T. (2002). *The feelings book.* Boston: Little, Brown, and Company.
This book covers a wide range of feelings, and has great illustrations.

Tolerance/Differences

Carter, M., & Santomauro, J. (2004). *Space travelers: An interactive program for developing social understanding social competence, and social skills for students with Asperger Syndrome, autism, and other social challenges.* Shawnee Mission, KS: Autism Asperger Publishing Company.
This book takes students on a journey through space where they learn social skills. Designed for older students (grades 4 and 5), it teaches self-regulation, problem solving, and stress release.

Carter, M., & Santomauro, J. (2007). *Pirates: An early years group program for developing social understanding and social competence for children with autism and related challenges.* Shawnee Mission, KS: Autism Asperger Publishing Company.
Based on a pirate theme, this program is designed for children aged preschool to third grade. It helps children with ASD to learn skills in emotional expression, making friends, and solving social problems.

Espin, R. (2003). *Amazingly ... Alphie.* Shawnee Mission, KS: Autism Asperger Publishing Company.
Alphie is a computer that is "wired differently," and has trouble fitting in. The book is written for slightly older children, and the focus is on accepting difference.

McCracken, H. (2006). *That's what is different about me! Helping children understand Autism Spectrum Disorders.* Shawnee Mission, KS: Autism Asperger Publishing Company.
This is a fun and interactive program that provides children with information about autism in an age-appropriate and sensitive manner. This packaged puppet program can be used by parents and teachers. DVD and coloring books available.

Meiners, C. (2006). *Accept and value each person.* Minneapolis, MN: Free Spirit Publishing.
This book introduces diversity, and encourages inclusion and acceptance. It also encourages children to appreciate the differences between people and the individual talents and characteristics of each person.

Meiners, C. (2006). *Reach out and give.* Minneapolis, MN: Free
Spirit Publishing.
*This book promotes generosity and helpfulness, and intro-
duces the concept of a circle of giving.*

Murrell, D. (2004). *Oliver Onion – The onion who learns to accept
and be himself.* Shawnee Mission, KS: Autism Asperger
Publishing Company.
*This book addresses issues faced by children with ASD and
other differences. The focus is on celebrating the uniqueness
of each person.*

Parr, T. (2001). *It's ok to be different.* Boston: Little, Brown, and Company.
*This book covers a wide range of differences that children can
relate to and encourages acceptance. It includes differences
such as baldness, needing glasses, using a wheelchair, being
adopted, and having an invisible friend. It also reviews that it
is fine to have a variety of basic feelings and that it is good to
behave in positive ways toward others. Specifics include doing acts of kindness, being kind to someone, feeling proud of
oneself, getting mad, and doing something nice for oneself.*

Specific Disabilities

Larson, E. M. (2006). *I am utterly unique: Celebrating the strengths of
children with Asperger Syndrome and high-functioning autism.*
Shawnee Mission, KS: Autism Asperger Publishing Company.
*This book, laid out in an A-to-Z format, celebrates the ex-
traordinary gifts and unique perspectives of children with
ASD. Each page of this playful alphabet book presents of one
of these children's many talents and abilities.*

Peralta, S. (2002). *All about my brother.* Shawnee Mission, KS: Autism Asperger Publishing Company.
This books helps typically developing children understand that a child with autism is a person that has unique interests and abilities. It is warmly written by a sibling.

Thompson, M. (1996.) *Andy and his yellow frisbee.* Bethesda, MD: Woodbine House.
This book describes the behaviors of a child with autism in a child-friendly and understanding way. It may help peers to understand the unique characteristics of a child on the autism spectrum.

Peer Training

In some cases, it is helpful to prepare peers to interact successfully with the student with HFA/AS. For example, it may help to get the student's attention before greeting her or asking her a question. In fact, this has been shown to be an effective strategy for siblings of children with autism (Celiberti & Harris, 1993). Peer training approaches have been highly successful, often with children with autism who have more significant deficits (e.g., Odom & Strain, 1986; Strain, 1983; Strain, Kerr, & Ragland, 1979).

Pivotal skills emphasized include establishing attention, providing prompts and feedback, and persisting in efforts to interact with others (e.g., Carr & Darcy, 1990; McGee, Almeida, Sulzer-Azaroff, & Feldman, 1992). Depending on the characteristics of the learner with HFA/AS, it may be helpful for peers to develop several of these skills. As noted in Chapter 4, it may make the interactions more successful, and it may decrease the likelihood that peers become discouraged in their attempts to interact.

One major limitation of this approach is the "natural" quality of this kind of training. Some schools, teams, or parents may feel that such training deviates from their vision of inclusion or stigmatizes the student in undesirable ways. Proximity to peers (in the absence of training), in and of itself, does not automatically produce positive social benefit.

Parents as Team Members

Many parents of students with HFA/AS have a long history of intense involvement in their children's educational program. This has helped their children to succeed, to master skills, and to make progress. In fact, the learning characteristics of children with ASD necessitate and encourage a high level of such involvement. Specifically, parental involvement ensures consistency in addressing learning problems or behavioral issues, assists in generalization of skills from one setting to another, and contributes to timely adjustments in instructional methods to facilitate learning and reduce frustration.

So, what strategies build effective collaboration with families? First of all, it is imperative that the parents' expertise about their child be recognized, respected, and incorporated into plans and strategies, whenever possible. Furthermore, many parents of children with HFA/AS are highly knowledgeable about ASD and about interventions. As discussed in Chapter 5, effective collaboration will enhance team functioning and learner outcome.

It is important to recognize that, as in any collaboration, there will be differences of opinion and awkward moments. Parents and educators may not agree about the best path to address a specific problem. This is especially likely to occur with children with HFA/AS, because these children are so different across settings and because their deficits can be both subtle and complex.

It is important to use these circumstances as opportunities to work toward solutions that take into account the information and experience of all parties. Many parents of students with special needs initially worry about an inclusive experience (Snell & Janney, 2000). However, most report that their children have more friends, more social interaction, and higher self-esteem as a result of the experience (Green & Shinn, 1994; Guralnick, Connor, & Hammond, 1995; Reichart et al., 1989).

Summary

Transition planning is a complex endeavor. It is important to train staff adequately to ensure success. Training should be learner-specific, and should include modeling and feedback on implementation. Such training is especially important for shadows assigned to work with individual students. This role is a broad one, and a well-trained and observant shadow can be a tremendous asset to both the student and the entire team. The needs of the student, his or her parents, the entire educational team, and potential classmates must be reviewed and integrated into the planning process. Furthermore, the classroom environment can be structured to minimize difficulty, provide support, and foster socialization. A checklist for assessing the presence of the essential components for success in transitioning appears in Table 3.6.

Table 3.6
Transition Checklist

CLASSROOM ENVIRONMENT

- ☐ Has the classroom environment been designed to minimize distractions?
- ☐ Has the classroom environment been designed to provide support (visual cues)?
- ☐ Are motivational systems in place to support classwide positive behavior?
- ☐ Are there transition signals?

HOME-SCHOOL CONNECTION

- ☐ Has someone been identified as the family liaison?
- ☐ Is there a communication system in place for family and staff (notebook, daily sheet)?
- ☐ Can information be shared with the family about upcoming lessons on a regular basis?
- ☐ Has the family been asked to share information about the child's specific interests, abilities, etc.?

TRAINING

- ☐ Is the training learner-specific?
- ☐ Does training include demonstration?
- ☐ Do staff receive regular feedback on implementation?
- ☐ Is the shadow being given individualized training?

GOAL ASSESSMENT

- ☐ Will supplementary social skills training be needed?
- ☐ Is there a plan to address social skill deficits?
- ☐ Will peer training be done?
- ☐ Have parents been involved in plans to educate peers?

In the next chapter, we will discuss the major treatment approaches for young students with HFA/AS. A great deal of attention will be given to ABA. Other treatments discussed include sensory-based interventions and social skills training approaches.

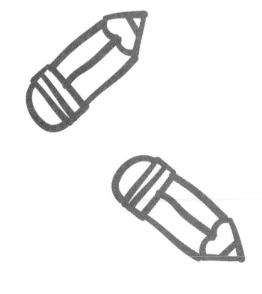

Chapter 4

TYPES OF INTERVENTION

Services for young children with HFA/AS have developed substantially over the past several years. It is very exciting to see the emergence of so many strategies and approaches that can help children succeed and build skills. At the same time, it can be overwhelming for parents and professionals to learn about each of these approaches and to incorporate them into their interactions with their students/children.

In addition to learning per se, in recent years, there has been an increased focus on ensuring that all students with disabilities undergo adequate and appropriate assessment and treatment of any behaviors that interfere with learning. The IDEA (Individuals with Disabilities Education Act) amendments of 1997 mandate that all students have a right to a functional assessment (see Chapter 2) of their challenging behaviors. Results of such an assessment are then used to guide the development of effective treatments for problem behaviors in school settings.

There has also been a great deal of emphasis in recent years on treating students with the highest levels of respect and dignity, including incorporating their preferences into instructional inter- actions, and on preventing behavioral escalations using a variety of environmental, curricular, and interpersonal supports. These strategies are often referred to as positive behavioral supports.

Further, in the realm of skill acquisition, there has been a great deal of interest in how we can help learners to more successfully navigate school expectations and environments. In addition, there is great in- terest in how we can efficiently teach skills, especially social skills.

In this chapter, we will discuss a number of interventions. For some of them (e.g., sensory integration), there is little empirical evi- dence of their effectiveness, despite a growing body of anecdotal reports. Other interventions are backed with substantial empirical support (e.g., applied behavior analysis [ABA]). We will also high- light some best practice strategies for working with individuals on the autism spectrum, such as using visual supports and making environmental adaptations to facilitate independence and im- prove behavior.

Environmental Navigation and Skill Acquisition

Many interventions may be used to build skills in preschoolers and young children with HFA/AS. In addition, a wide variety of sup- ports may be used across different types of intervention to meet their unique needs. Thus, teachers use a variety of environmental, visual, and instructional supports to help learners to navigate their environments and to comprehend expectations. A summary of effective strategies in these domains is provided in Table 4.1.

Table 4.1
Types of Strategies Used with Young Children with HFA/AS

ENVIRONMENTAL STRATEGIES

Place learner away from significant distractors

Place learner near the teacher

Place learner near appropriate peer models

Reduce excess visual and auditory distractions

VISUAL STRATEGIES

Provide a clear visual schedule for the day

Provide mini-schedules for activities

Provide visually based step-by-step instructions for multi-component tasks

Label learner's cubby and areas of classroom (with pictures and/or words)

Use motivational systems that provide visual information on earning rewards

INSTRUCTIONAL SUPPORTS

Simplify language used during instruction

Pair difficult tasks with easier tasks

Break tasks up into several subtasks

Teach in briefer chunks of time (with access to breaks)

Provide information in child's strongest modality

Provide information visually when possible

Allow learner to answer in preferred modality

Incorporate preferred materials

Use transitional cues

Highlight strengths

Use cooperative learning

Use observational learning

Use clear motivational systems

Use self-monitoring aids

Specific approaches to helping learners with HFA/AS include sensory integration therapy, applied behavior analysis (ABA), social communication training, social skill training programs, and problem-solving training. The goals, methods, and applications of these approaches will be extensively reviewed in this chapter. Sensory integration intervention targets the abnormalities in sensory processing that can affect behavior in all contexts. While there is not a body of research supporting the effectiveness of sensory integration intervention, its relevance and importance to particular learners can be substantial (e.g., Myles et al., 2000).

ABA has tremendous relevance for addressing the skill deficits in preschoolers with AS and HFA. While discrete trial instruction and other methods within ABA are not as relevant or appropriate for many of these learners due to their reduced need for repetition and their ability to learn in less formal contexts, the more naturalistic strategies within ABA, such as incidental teaching, can address problems in initiation, spontaneity, and the pragmatic use of language.

Fluency within ABA has recently been discussed (Fabrizio & Moors, 2003; Weiss, 2001, 2005) as an area that has been inadequately emphasized with learners with ASD. Fluency focuses on the rate of skill demonstration (i.e., how rapidly someone can engage in a behavior). Taking too long to respond to peers or to teachers can be construed as dysfluent. Therefore, addressing ease and speed of skill demonstration may make a learner more successful in interactions with peers and in group learning environments. Functional assessment and functional analyses of challenging behaviors have become essential, and are even mandated by law. An ABA approach to challenging behaviors is entirely consistent with positive behavioral supports and with student-centered interventions.

Many social communication and social skill training programs have been developed to address the social difficulties of learners on the autism spectrum. Many of these approaches target deficits in understanding social situations and in solving social problems.

Sensory Integration Therapy

Sensory integration (SI) has been defined as the ability to internally organize sensory input. SI theory posits that many children on the autism spectrum have difficulty receiving and processing sensory information (Ayres, 1979). For example, some students appear to be extremely *hypersensitive* to sensory input, and may be bothered by noise, lighting, smells, tastes, and textures. Other students are *hyposensitive* to sensory input, and may not react as expected, even to input such as pain. In response to SI dysfunction, children may seek extra sensory input and be oversensitive to sensory aspects of the environment and underresponsive to sensory input (Simpson, 2005).

Three main sensory systems are emphasized by SI theorists: the proprioceptive (muscles and joints), vestibular (balance), and tactile (touch) systems. For example, a vestibular problem might manifest itself as a person having difficulty knowing where his body is in space. Determining and accommodating information about speed and movement would be vestibular-related skills. Proprioception is related to body awareness and how certain body parts are moving. Tactile input determines how texture, pressure, heat, cold, and pain are experienced. See Table 4.2 for a summary of some sensory dysregulation problems common to autism.

Table 4.2 Common Sensory Dysregulation Problems in Children with HFA/AS	
SENSORY SYSTEM	**DYSREGULATION**
Proprioceptive	Body awareness problems
	• Difficulties with coordinating body movement
Vestibular	Understanding body in space
Tactile	Experiencing texture, pressure, temperature, pain

As mentioned, there is a paucity of empirical data on SI intervention, although anecdotal reports of its success abound, and belief in its impact is strong. Supporters of this approach claim major benefits, including improved sensory organization. It is difficult to substantiate such claims, because we cannot objectively measure its impact (i.e., sensory integration is not associated with one area of the brain, which we could measure to assess the impact of intervention).

KATHLEEN had ongoing issues with fidgeting and wandering in class. Her parents had noted that she always seemed to need "regular exercise" to stay calm and focused, and the educational team had anecdotally reported that she seemed to focus better after activities such as outdoor recess.

They decided to investigate whether, in fact, regular access to certain activities would improve her ability to attend. They took some data on Kathleen's ability to attend to get an initial measure of her skills in this area. Then they began to give her 15 minutes per hour of gross-motor activities recommended by the occupational therapist. They continued to take data on her ability to attend, and then met as a team to review the data. As it turned out, the new plan increased Kathleen's ability to attend by about 50%. They also noted that it had other positive effects, including a reduction in her hand play.

Due to the general lack of empirical evidence in this area, it has been suggested that clinicians and teachers take data on how SI procedures benefit a particular learner (Simpson, 2005). For example, it can be immensely helpful to methodically evaluate how SI intervention assists learners in their behavior, attention, and learning. Some often hypothesized benefits to sensory interventions include:

- Reduced rates of stereotyped or self-stimulatory behaviors

- Improved capacity for verbal imitation

- Improved attention

- Improved engagement

Staff members can assess the impact of such interventions (which include brushing, swinging, and regular access to physical activities) by collecting data on the behaviors most expected to change. This is often done by taking samples of data before and after such sessions, and comparing the rates of the behaviors. For example, teachers might collect information on the frequency of self-stimulatory behavior in the half hour before an SI session and in the half-hour following an SI session. Alternately, they might record whether the behavior is happening at the end of each minute for those two half-hour sessions. Such data enable a comparison of behavior before and after sensory treatment.

From a sensory perspective, both assessment of sensory needs and treatment of sensory issues are essential components of effective intervention for children on the autism spectrum. Sensory interventions can include regular access to sensory input activities, replacement of sensory-based activities with more acceptable outlets that serve the same sensory function, compensatory and coping strategies to facilitate adaptation in difficult sensory circumstances, and ongoing assessment of sensory needs.

Applied Behavior Analysis (ABA)

This section will include a description of instructional approaches that are part of applied behavior analysis, which has been shown to be the most effective intervention for individuals with ASD. We will begin with a discussion of some common misconceptions of ABA, and then review the most common ABA teaching strategies. Instructional strategies reviewed will include discrete trial instruction and the naturalistic strategies such as incidental teaching. In addition, the concept of fluency and its implications for learners on the spectrum will be reviewed. Finally, we will discuss the process of functional assessment and how it helps to understand and effectively treat challenging behaviors.

There are many misconceptions about ABA, especially when it comes to individuals on the autism spectrum who are higher functioning. It is commonly assumed that such individuals do not need ABA, and that their skills are beyond the scope of typical ABA interventions. It is also commonly thought that ABA has nothing to offer outside of traditional discrete trial instruction (DTI), a form of sequenced instruction that uses repetition to aid learning (Koegel, Russo, & Rincover, 1977).

While it is true that many higher functioning individuals on the spectrum do not need DTI, nevertheless, for some, it can have relevance for a brief period of time or to teach specific skills. Current DTI instruction is quite different from its original applications, focusing on the use of errorless learning procedures (Etzel & LeBlanc, 1979; Lancioni & Smeets, 1986; Terrace, 1963; Touchette & Howard, 1984), to reduce repeated errors and error patterns, and task interspersal.

Task interspersal, which involves mixing new instructional targets with mastered material, has been demonstrated to be more effective than massed practice (in which the same item is practiced over and over again) of new items (Dunlap, 1984; Koegel & Koegel, 1995). In this way, instruction is more naturalistic, as students are not asked to engage in the same behavior or respond to the same request over and over again. As such, it better prepares learners for how teachers will interact with them throughout their educational career, and it prevents students from automatically responding or responding without attending to the language of the instruction.

When carried out using these procedures, DTI can build skills very effectively, particularly in certain content areas (imitation, matching, vocabulary building, pre-academics) or when intrinsic motivation for the content is low (such as when a child does not enjoy a task like handwriting and finds it unpleasant). It is also sometimes easier to teach groups using naturalistic methods, as they are well suited to thematic discussions in group activities. Table 4.3 shows an example of naturalistic task interspersal.

Table 4.3
Example of Naturalistic Task Interspersal

The teacher may discuss zoo animals with the entire group. She may target receptive identification of animal pictures, expressive identification of animal pictures, and receptive and expressive identification of animals by their features, animal sounds, animal habitats, and categories of animals. Sample questions asked of students might include:

- Touch the giraffe, elephant, lion, monkey, hippo, penguin, flamingo, bear, snake

- What is the name of this animal?

- Can you find the one with the long neck?

In this example, the teacher covers a range of receptive and expressive language skills. The approach also allows her to individualize instruction for children at differing levels of ability.

ABA strategies with more broad relevance to HFA/AS students include all the naturalistic strategies within ABA. Targeting initiation, language use, spontaneity, and the generalization of skills, these approaches are characterized by the hallmark characteristics of ABA: a theoretical embeddedness in learning theory, a focus on the use of empirically validated techniques, the targeting of specific instructional goals, the use of methodical teaching strategies, data collection to guide instruction and to assess the impact of instructional efforts, dynamic data-driven programming (with rapid adjustments in response to learner struggles), and a focus on the generalization of skills as part of what defines successful teaching (Harris & Weiss, 2007; Weiss, 2005).

When many people read about ABA intervention, they realize that they have seen many elements of it in place, even when it has not been called ABA. Good teachers use many ABA strategies as part of their daily interactions with students. For example, they provide positive feedback for good performance, they provide encouragement when things are difficult, they make tasks easier to enable students to succeed, and they plan lessons in a way that facilitates the transfer of skills. They also observe how their students are doing, and alter their instructional strategy when student performance warrants it. Table 4.4 lists ABA strategies commonly used.

Table 4.4
ABA Strategies Commonly Used by Effective Teachers

- Reinforcement

- Encouragement/coaching

- Modification of demands to facilitate student success and reduce frustration

- Assessment of student performance in an ongoing way

- Alteration of expectations based on student performance

Naturalistic Methodologies

ABA strives to make socially significant and meaningful changes for learners (Cooper et al., 1987, 2007). Naturalistic strategies help in achieving those goals by focusing on the demonstration of skills in the natural environment and in the absence of assistance from instructors.

Incidental teaching. One of the more widespread forms of naturalistic ABA instruction is incidental teaching. Hart and Risley (1982) defined incidental teaching as a procedure "used to get elaborated language by waiting for another person to initiate conversation about a topic and then responding in ways that ask for more language from that person" (p. 5). The goal of incidental teaching is elaboration. Thus, the procedures help to get more language from the child and to prolong, strengthen, and expand the communication. Common everyday examples of incidental teaching procedures abound. In fact, many teachers and others utilize the approach without labeling it as such, as it has become part of best practice instruction, especially for learners with language deficits.

For example, teachers sometimes place desired objects out of a student's reach, but in a conspicuous spot. Such a strategy sets the occasion for working on elaboration. If a child reaches toward the object and says, "ball," the teacher can say, "Tell me, I want the blue ball." When the student provides that sentence, she gets access to the ball. The steps of incidental teaching (see Table 4.5) include arranging a setting that contains materials of interest to the child, waiting for the child to initiate an interaction about an object of interest, asking for more elaborate language or approximations to speech, and providing the object for which the child initiated (Fenske, Krantz, & McClannahan, 2001).

Table 4.5
Steps of Incidental Teaching

Arranging the setting
- High-interest items visible but not accessible

Waiting for an initiation
- Interaction or request about desired/preferred item

Asking for an elaboration
- Requiring more communication/language

Providing the object
- Contingent upon the more elaborate response

Important elements of incidental teaching include the focus on initiation. That is, the learner's interest determines that there will be a teaching moment. As illustrated in Table 4.6, this is very different from traditional types of ABA instruction, in which the teacher determines when and what will be taught in a lesson. Further, the behavior that is strengthened is initiation. This is a major strength, as DTI stresses and largely builds responsivity in learners. That is, incidental teaching and the other naturalistic ABA strategies, such as pivotal response training, natural language paradigm, and natural environment training, balance the focus on responding to an instructor with a focus on communicating wants and needs independently and spontaneously (without help, hints, or directions from a teacher).

Table 4.6
Comparison of Discrete Trial Instruction and Incidental Teaching

METHOD	INITIATOR	FOCUS	PLANNING	REPETITIVE?
DTI	Teacher	Responsivity	Formal	Highly
IT	Child	Initiation	Informal	No
		Elaboration	Opportunity-based	

In incidental teaching, the child's interests create the opportunity for teaching. The teacher is assured that the learner is motivated. Thus, a teacher who is using incidental teaching will be continually on the lookout for opportunities to create teaching moments. It requires that the teacher respond to naturally occurring opportunities in ways that facilitate language. Capitalizing on these informal teaching moments, teachers build language that is generalized more easily and that occurs more spontaneously.

The applications of incidental teaching go well beyond simple requesting. It can also be used to build conversational skills. Specifically, it is used to elaborate an exchange on a topic that is of interest to the student. It can also be used to target sentence structure and the complexity of communication (Fenske et al., 2001), and to help learners use adjectives and prepositions, and ask for assistance or ask questions. For example, a child can be prompted to specify size (e.g., when asking for a cracker) or color (e.g., when asking for a crayon). Similarly, a child can be helped to ask for help (e.g., when presented with an impossible task) or to ask for information (e.g., about where an item is if the child needs it and it is not visible).

This focus on initiation is important because many students with HFA/AS struggle in this realm. They may passively wait for assistance from a teacher or peer. They may not respond to their own needs or to environmental cues without help or support from others. Being able to articulate desires is essential. That is, it is not enough for students to be good responders; they must also be good initiators. This is particularly important in navigating mainstream educational environments, where teachers are not so available to anticipate needs or wants.

Pivotal response training and natural language paradigm. Other naturalistic strategies include pivotal response training and natural language paradigm (e.g., Koegel & Koegel, 2005; Koegel, Koegel, & Surrat, 1992; Koegel, O'Dell, & Koegel, 1987; Laski, Charlop, & Schreibman, 1988). Both of these approaches emphasize teaching in natural contexts, especially in play. They also emphasize following the child's lead, using high-interest materials, and teaching language in the context of child-preferred activities.

For example, an ABA instructor using a naturalistic approach with a child who loves garages and cars might work on the concepts of "up" and "down" while playing with the child on the floor with a garage toy with ramps. The child could learn these concepts in the context of the preferred activity of moving the cars up and down the ramps. The interactions in such naturalistic approaches are playful and informal, lacking the structure and formality of discrete trial instruction. It is much more likely, therefore, that skills will have meaning for the learner and will generalize to other situations.

Natural environment training. The most recent of the naturalistic ABA approaches (Sundberg & Partington, 1998), natural environment training, like natural language paradigm and pivotal response training, emphasizes taking the child's lead, using intrinsically motivating materials, and teaching in natural environments and contexts. Like incidental teaching, it emphasizes initiation as an important class of behavior to target.

Natural environment training also adds a unique aspect of instruction: the use of the verbal behavior (VB) language classification system. The VB classification system, developed by Skinner (1957), focused on the functions of expressive language. Skinner discussed the importance of mands (requests), tacts (comments), intraverbals (to-and-from conversational exchanges), and echoics (verbal imitation). All of these are areas of deficit for most learners on the autism spectrum. Manding, in particular, is weak in many children with ASD.

It can be very helpful to target manding in learners with HFA/AS who exhibit deficits in spontaneous requesting. Manding is often initially targeted in special sessions, in which very enticing and interesting items are available to the learner upon request. In general, no other demands are placed on learners during manding sessions. The sole goal is to increase spontaneous requests. Learners generally enjoy these sessions, associate teachers with the reinforcers available, and become more independent and more elaborate in their requests over time.

Manding is also a long-term curricular emphasis, as requesting skills can expand well beyond asking for objects and activities to include requests for information, for an object necessary to initiate or complete a task, for help with a difficult task, for a break when task demands are too high, or for attention from a teacher (Partington & Sundberg 1998). When conceptualized broadly, manding has tremendous relevance. For example, an effective mander can tell a teacher when she needs something, can ask for more information when a direction is not completely understood, and can request appropriately for a reduction in demands when she feels frustrated.

Teaching the other functions of manding (e.g., manding for help, attention, and escape from a demand) often helps to reduce behavioral difficulties. Students may be taught to mand for attention or escape in contrived situations, in which they are prompted to mand. A teacher may present an extremely difficult non-preferred task and prompt the student to ask for a break (escape). Similarly, the teacher may reduce her attention by interacting with another student. Someone may then prompt the child to request, "play with me."

Such strategies help the student to feel a sense of control over his environment and teach him that using language to request will get results. In such an environment, the need to resort to disruptive behavior to get one's needs met is seriously reduced, and more adaptive behaviors replace challenging behaviors.

The social relevance of naturalistic strategies. It is also very helpful to teach conversational skills in naturalized contexts. It much better prepares learners for conversations in their natural environments and for the diversity in topics and responses they are likely to encounter. One of the criticisms of DTI approaches to language development has been that they fail to mirror daily life in natural environments. This is true, especially in the context of conversation. Conversation, in real life, is not scripted or repetitive. People ask things in many different ways and in combination with other topics. To succeed in conversation, therefore, learners need to be flexible – both about listening to their conversational partners and about answering questions posed to them. To the extent possible, the learner should be taught conversation in naturalistic ways.

Fluency: A Concept with Social Consequences

In an everyday sense, we are all fluent at many things. Fluency has been defined as the combination of speed and accuracy that defines competent performance (Binder, 1996). Think for a moment of all the things you can do easily and well, such as making a sandwich, driving a car, and getting dressed. When someone is fluent at something, he or she can do it easily and fast.

Many individuals with HFA/AS demonstrate dysfluent skills, which makes them discrepant from their peers and may lead to missed opportunities for socialization. One major aspect of non-fluent responding is the rate at which a child engages in a behavior. She may be perfectly accurate, but slow. If it takes a student 15 minutes to do a matching worksheet that the rest of the class completes in 5 minutes, the student will be out of sync with the classroom schedule and pace.

Further, dysfluency has social ramifications. For example, if peers greet a student with HFA/AS, they will wait briefly for a reply. If the student with HFA/AS takes too long to reply, the peer will typically exit, because (a) he has lost interest, (b) he assumes he is not going to get a response, or (c) he got distracted by other things. This is a very common scenario, especially in the preschool and early elementary years, when most peers have short attention spans.

In group learning contexts such as circle time, long latencies to respond pose similar problems. A teacher might call on the student with HFA/AS with a question she knows is easy for the child. She can wait a brief period for a reply. However, as the seconds mount, she has to move on. She may have 22 other children she is in danger of losing, so she politely moves on. Again, it is not uncommon in this scenario for the student to ultimately reply, but after a lag time that is exceedingly long.

Students who exhibit long latencies to respond miss social opportunities and group learning opportunities. Furthermore, their peers may make unjustified assumptions about them. They may think that the student who didn't respond doesn't like them, isn't interested in playing, doesn't know the answer, or can't talk.

ABA clinicians have historically paid little attention to rate of response. Instead, accuracy has been the gold standard. In fact, there have been assumptions about the limitations of individuals on the autism spectrum regarding speed of response. Because so many students on the spectrum are apraxic (e.g., have difficulties planning their motor responses), long response latencies have been accepted and expected. However, it may well be the case that many individuals on the spectrum can respond more quickly.

Fluency-based instruction has focused on response rate with other populations for many years, but has only recently been extended to the population of learners with ASD (e.g., Fabrizio & Moors, 2003). Fluency proponents emphasize that there are benefits to achieving fluency that have major relevance to this population. For example, skills may generalize readily, students may be able to engage in skills for longer and in the face of distraction, and skill maintenance may be easier (e.g., Dougherty & Johnston, 1996).

Whether or not clinicians choose to do fluency-based instruction or simply focus on rate and latency as socially significant issues, there is benefit to incorporating this focus into instruction. Fluency may be targeted in several different ways, as outlined in Table 4.7.

Table 4.7
Ways to Target Fluency

ADDRESSING CORE MOTOR DEFICITS

- Assess rate of basic motor movement skills (6+6 component skills, such as reach, point, tap, etc.)

- Build speed of response to target levels

- Assess impact on composite skills

BUILDING SPEED OF RESPONSE WITH MASTERED MATERIALS

- Teach skills for accuracy first

- Build speed of response after acquisition

ENSURING SKILL IS AVAILABLE

- Use latency as the measurement of behavior, especially useful in group and social situations

- Address latency to response to teacher direction

- Address latency to social response

Functional Assessment and Functional Analysis

As discussed in Chapter 2, functional assessment has become mandatory and universal in addressing challenging behaviors. This reflects a positive shift from reducing behaviors to understanding behaviors and developing interventions based on such understanding.

Challenging behaviors do not occur without reason or in a vacuum. Children engage in challenging behaviors as a communication tool. We need to understand why the individual is exhibiting a specific behavior. Reducing the extent to which behaviors interfere with learning requires attention to what *function* a behavior serves. Interventions subsequently include finding and teaching effective replacement skills; that is, adaptive skills that serve the same function. In other words, if a student has been ripping up worksheets to get out of doing them (to escape), we can teach the student to request a break instead. The student still gets to escape a difficult task, but in a socially appropriate way. A longer-term strategy can include helping the child to tolerate difficult tasks or to request assistance, but immediately the focus may be on helping her to escape in a more appropriate way.

Teaching replacement skills generally requires contriving situations and prompting children to engage in the behavior the adult would like them to engage in instead of the targeted challenging behavior. For example, a student may be given a non-preferred worksheet, and then immediately be prompted to hand the teacher a break card and be asked to say, "Break, please." Over time, break cards may be made available (e.g., placed on desk or on clipboard). Teachers may remind the student by pointing to a break card or otherwise providing a subtle cue, "What can you say if you want a break?"

Functional assessment strategies also focus a great deal on antecedent intervention, or prevention of challenging behaviors. Using the example of the worksheet, it may be that a student would be much less likely to rip up worksheets if they were presented as matching vs. fill-in-the-blank. It may be that the student would be able to do two problems on a worksheet, but not 10. Or it may be that the student would be less likely to rip up the paper if the teacher was nearby during the lesson.

In many ways, when we understand the function of a behavior, we also come to understand how we can create an environment in which the likelihood of the behavior is extremely low. Adapting the environment to provide sufficient supports, modifying tasks, and increasing reinforcement are all strategies to prevent the occurrence of challenging behaviors.

Treating a challenging behavior requires a multi-layered approach with many elements. It is never a simple fix, and good intervention always entails multiple treatment approaches. The following scenario illustrates the diversity of approaches that characterizes such intervention.

BOBBY was having difficulty in school. Whenever it was time for learning center, he became disruptive. He tore his worksheets, he cried and screamed, he asked to go home, and he hit the teacher. The teachers had been removing him to the hallway, where they helped him to calm down by counting to 10. However, data trends showed that these disruptive episodes were increasing in intensity and in frequency. (The weekly average had increased from 3 to 8, and the intensity ratings by the teacher were nearly always severe.)

A functional assessment included interviews, observation, and ABC (antecedent-behavior-consequence) data. It seemed clear that there were two functions of Bobby's behavior. The primary function was escape. Bobby engaged in these behaviors to get out of learning centers. It also seemed that Bobby was seeking more 1:1 attention, which he invariably received when he became agitated. Staff members wanted to address both functions.

In order to address the escape function, several elements of intervention were put in place. First, Bobby was provided with easier and simpler tasks during learning centers. Instead of practicing the Handwriting Without Tears protocol, which he disliked, he was given matching tasks. Some of the matching tasks had letters on them, but they also contained pictures (which he highly preferred). Furthermore, the tasks were interspersed. Instead of working on pattern identification with blocks for 10 minutes as the other children did, Bobby worked on pattern identification for 2 minutes, and then engaged in more preferred activities for a minute before returning to pattern identification. Finally, Bobby was given a replacement skill (a break card) that he could use to get out of centers. At first, staff prompted him to use the card immediately upon coming to centers, and then when he began to get slightly agitated.

To address the attention function, staff built in more opportunities for 1:1 for Bobby. Each hour, Bobby could take a short walk or play a game with a staff member. They also worked on building Bobby's skills in requesting attention from others and in waiting for teacher attention in small groups.

Finally, Bobby received a great deal of reinforcement for appropriate behavior. He began a token system (in which he earned pennies as a concrete reminder of his progress toward earning a larger reward of computer time) that targeted his ability to stay in the group and do his work.

Positive Behavioral Supports

An extension of ABA that has taken functional assessment to another level is positive behavioral supports (PBS). PBS supports the use of multi-component interventions that include manipulating antecedents to prevent behavioral escalations and teaching alternative skills (Dunlap et al., 2000). The emphasis in PBS is on making significant and lasting outcomes for the child and for members of his or her family and larger community (Kincaid, Knoster, Harrower, Shannon, & Bustamante, 2002). As within other aspects of ABA, there is a strong focus on teaching socially desirable behaviors, not just behavior reduction.

PBS interventionists also target global quality-of-life issues and attend very rigorously to issues of social validation (i.e., is this difference meaningful?). That is, PBS interventionists want to know if the child is experiencing more happiness, more social connection, more preferred activities, and more community engagement as a result of changes in behavior. They are concerned with self-determination, and seek more integration of the person into his or her treatment decisions. The major value of PBS is that it is person-centered. Thus, normalization and inclusion are themes that prominently and frequently surface in the PBS literature.

Addressing Social Deficits Through ABA and Other Strategies

As mentioned earlier, the social deficits of ASD are substantial. Even students with HFA/AS who do extremely well in many other aspects of life struggle substantially in this realm. Major difficulties include social initiation, social responsiveness, and social comprehension.

A number of strategies within ABA address social skill deficits. In addition, several sister disciplines such as education, school psychology, and speech-language pathology have come up with strategies that are compatible with ABA interventions, such as Social Stories™. When social skills are addressed through ABA, there are clear targets of instruction, methodical teaching strategies, and data-based decision making.

In the next section, we will explore how ABA addresses skill deficits in social initiation, social responsiveness, and social comprehension. We will discuss the strategies commonly used to address these deficits.

Social initiations. ABA focuses on social initiations in an intensive manner. This is important, because without special attention, deficits in this area generally do not abate. Social initiations are key to opening doors for social relationships, an important survival skill for school. We have already discussed two strategies with relevance to initiation training: incidental teaching and mand training. Other aspects of initiation might be addressed directly, including greetings, asking questions, joining activities, commenting, and joint attention.

Joining an activity is important to target, as often students with HFA/AS fail to initiate in clear or effective ways. For example, they may stand on the sidelines and watch peers playing while peers have no idea that they would like to join. It may be helpful to first teach this skill with an instructor. While this approach lacks a fully natural quality, it does allow for teaching in a context where we can control many variables, including the response of the potential play partner(s). Eventually, the student must be prepared for the diversity of possibilities likely to be encountered, including refusal. When generalizing the skill to peers, it is helpful to initially introduce particularly willing peers into training.

MILLIE was very scared about joining social situations. She usually just watched from a distance. Even when peers asked her to join, she sometimes panicked, failed to answer, or ran away. Initially, teachers worked 1:1 with her in analog situations with highly preferred treats and activities. They gradually built her ability to ask to be part of a game or activity.

They worried about the transfer to peers, however, especially because Millie was so sensitive. Ruthie was a peer who was very sensitive and quiet, and who Millie was not afraid of. They initially had Ruthie join the analog situation with the teacher, slowly fading out the teacher's presence until Ruthie and Millie were interacting only with each other.

Another type of initiation training is initiating by *asking about another's ongoing activity*. Typically developing peers do this a lot. For example, they ask a friend, "What are you coloring?" or "What are you building?" Children with HFA/AS are unlikely to inquire about a peer's project. Teaching them this skill can open the door to other social exchanges. Peers usually feel flattered, and usually respond positively to such inquiries. Furthermore, it sometimes results in a transition to a parallel or cooperative play situation.

A variation on the above activity is to teach children with HFA/AS to *comment on the activities of others*. They can comment on or narrate what they see other children doing (e.g., "That's a cool house." Or "The firefighter is putting out the fire."). There are many opportunities for commenting in the daily school lives of young children, including free play, play centers, art activities, or block building.

A special kind of initiation that is often absent even among socially aware children on the autism spectrum is requests for *joint attention.* At the most basic level, requests for joint attention include asking someone to look at or notice something that you are looking at or noticing. It involves the sharing of experience. This is something that typically developing learners do from a very young age with no training or encouragement.

Joint attention is becoming an increased focus of many interventions targeted to individuals on the autism spectrum, including ABA. It can be taught directly, through contrived experiences that mirror real-life situations. The real issue with teaching joint attention is the extent to which such instruction generalizes to natural contexts. This is largely an unanswered question, about which more data may become available in the next few years.

Social responsiveness. Social responsiveness is also critically important for social success. If we do not address social responsiveness, we run the risk that others' initiations are not reinforced by our students, leading to lack of reciprocity and social isolation. We want to help our learners be responsive to the interest and inquiries of others. Skills often targeted within ABA interventions include greetings and farewells, social questions, responding to the initiations of others, and maintaining a conversation.

Greetings and farewells are important, as they indicate and promote social awareness. Responding to social questions and to the invitations of others is also important, because we do not want peers to stop making those types of overtures as often happens when they fail to get responses. Sustaining conversations is important in building, lengthening, and expanding the types of interactions that learners have with their peers. Some strategies that can assist in this regard include teaching students to offer similar information, to ask questions, and to follow up on comments (not just questions).

TAKU was pretty good at answering direct questions from peers. If someone asked him what he did on the weekend, he might talk about playing in the snow or watching a movie. However, he often missed social opportunities because he did not offer similar information. If David talked about playing in the snow, Taku would listen. However, unless David asked him something specific, he did not offer any information. This is a pattern common to many individuals on the autism spectrum. They do not perceive comments or information sharing as social opportunities.

Teachers began working with Taku to teach him to respond with similar information. They would contrive conversations and prompt him to offer similar information. (Teacher: "I had a snowball fight with my brother this weekend." Taku: "We made a giant igloo.") At first, these conversational exchanges were scripted. Over time, however, teachers were able to simply use an expectant look to get Taku to generate similar information, and ultimately, it was also possible to fade this prompt out.

Social comprehension. Social comprehension is the most abstract area of social skills training, and the area in which deficits among individuals on the autism spectrum can be most extreme. Social comprehension is comprised of many multi-element and abstract skills, including following social rules (i.e., understanding and doing what is expected in a given context) and understanding and acting on social nuances. A variety of strategies are commonly used by behavior analysts in targeting these skills. These strategies include Social Stories™ (which will be addressed later in this chapter), rule cards, providing feedback on performance, role-plays, and video instruction.

Rule cards (see samples in Figure 4.1) are essentially a behavioral/ cognitive rehearsal opportunity that can be helpful in teaching students to follow social rules associated with a particular activity or to follow a general social rule (such as sharing). A rule card clearly states the objectives for a particular activity, and can be presented as text, a picture cue, or both. Often a rule card can be presented to the entire class, although it is also possible to create and/or present a rule card for just one child.

SHARING

When a friend asks for a toy I am playing with ...
- I can say, "Here."
- I can give the toy to my friend.

When I want a turn with a toy, I can ask a friend.

RULES FOR THE MEDIA CENTER

In the media center ...
- I need to wait for the teacher to assign me a computer.

- I need to finish my assigned work before I play games.

- When I am finished with my assigned work, I can raise my hand for the teacher.

- The teacher will check my work.

- Then I can play games on the computer until class is over.

Figure 4.1. Sample rule cards.

The use of rule cards is usually combined with behavioral rehearsal techniques.

MRS. JONES read the rule card on sharing developed for a preschool class to a small group of preschoolers and then queried them for comprehension. She then contrived a practice opportunity, in which she had insufficient numbers of toys.

She presented two scooters for three children. Two children were given scooters, and the third was urged to request a scooter from one of the other children. The child asked was assisted to respond "here" and to give the scooter to his friend. He, in turn, asked the third friend for a scooter. Multiple practice opportunities with scooters were followed by more practice with balls. Much reinforcement was provided for remembering the rule card and for sharing with friends. Initially, the type of assistance given was substantial (presenting and reading the card, reminding the child of the script). Later in the activity, the teacher simply occasionally said, "Remember the rule card." Reinforcement in the form of verbal praise was used whenever any of the children followed the rule card.

Role-plays can also be used to address deficits in social comprehension. In particular, role-plays may be used to target nuances of interaction that are difficult for the child to understand in the context of social interaction, such as the need to maintain the topic of conversation. Many formats work effectively to target social deficits in this way. The instructor can use characters or puppets to demonstrate a social exchange. In such a format, the child is an observer, and has opportunities to identify appropriate social skills. Alternately, a scenario can be enacted with people, including the instructor and possibly the child. In this format, the child can assume a participatory role, which provides opportunities for the child to directly practice the target skills.

Items to focus on in role-plays include orientation to the speaker, eye contact with a conversational partner, engaging in appropriate conversation, responding to common occurrences, being assertive, and managing frustration. Appropriate conversational targets might include skills such as engaging in contextually appropriate language and consistently responding. This can be very helpful for students who either occasionally are oblivious to the conversational overtures of others or who respond in idiosyncratic ways (e.g., scripting from movies or discussing their own high-interest topics instead of the topic at hand).

MICHAEL often put off his preschool peers because of his scripting. No one understood what he was talking about, and several of the kids began avoiding him. His typical response to a morning greeting would be to say, "There's a snake in my boots," scripting from Toy Story.

To help Michael to understand appropriate and inappropriate responses to social overtures, role-plays were used. Michael played the observer role, watching a scenario enacted. Teachers had him identify if the response was appropriate and had him practice a more pro-social response.

Scenarios could also include frequent classroom situations such as a friend getting hurt, a friend asking for help, a person sneezing, and so on. Extending role-plays to assertiveness and frustration helps to provide specific information on how to manage emotions and respond in a socially appropriate way even when angry or disappointed. Table 4.8 shows sample role-play targets.

Table 4.8
Sample Role-Play Targets

- Making eye contact with your conversational partner
- Orienting to a play/conversational partner
- Appropriate body use during conversation
- Speaking at an appropriate volume
- Responding contextually
- Responding to someone's request
- Responding to another's distress
- Asserting oneself appropriately
- Managing frustration

Providing Feedback on Performance

Feedback on performance may be provided in the context of be-havioral rehearsal strategies used with rule cards and in role-plays. Feedback may be given in the moment, as suggested in the rule card example above. For example, students can be helped to dem-onstrate the more pro-social response in the moment.

Feedback can also be given in a delayed manner. Here students are asked to discuss and review a circumstance that happened earlier in the day or week, and review and practice appropriate alternate responses in a post-hoc fashion. Generally, teachers se-lect real-life scenarios that actually occurred, and for which there are many appropriate potential responses.

Video. Video can also be used as a medium to provide feedback to a student on performance of a skill or on general adherence to behavioral rules. Since many learners on the autism spectrum have visual strengths, they tend to respond positively to the use of video as an instructional medium. Besides, it provides very concrete and clear examples of target issues (as opposed to conversations, which can be much more abstract).

If a student is struggling with understanding what the expectations are in circle time, for example, it can be helpful to use video to instruct as well as to provide feedback. For instructional purposes, you might want to select a particularly good example of a peer. In exposing the target child to the video, you can review the expectations and have the child indicate whether the model is fulfilling them.

This strategy can eventually be extended to a self-evaluation process. That is, the student could watch tapes of herself, and answer questions about how well she is following the circle time rules. This is sometimes a good beginning to self-monitoring and self-management, which have major implications for independence and generalization.

Rehearsal. Video can also be an excellent means of providing opportunities for rehearsing appropriate behavior. One of the challenges within a school day is to find enough opportunities to practice specific skills, such as sitting in circle time. Some learners make more rapid progress if more opportunities to practice skills are provided. For example, a teacher can be taped during circle time, and the student can watch the tape at home. In this way, the student can practice the skill more often than the circumstance naturally occurs.

If such a strategy is used, there may also be opportunities to focus on good models. That is, the focus can be on a peer who listens well, raises her hand, keeps her eyes on the teacher, and sits quietly. This could eventually be extended to a peer buddy system. A buddy might sit with the target student and actively model appropriate behavior. A teacher might provide direct reinforcement to the peer model for appropriate behavior. Focusing on socially appropriate models highlights the most important aspects of the target, and helps to build peer imitation skills.

Other Targets of Intervention Using ABA
ABA can also address other social deficits through systematic teaching and data collection. Areas that might be targeted through systematic instruction include humor, nonverbal communication, perspective taking, joint attention, and problem solving. Deficits in these areas are considerable for most children with HFA/AS, and can impede the extent to which they are successful and/or comfortable in socially integrated settings.

Lack of humor. Understanding humor is very difficult, and takes time and maturation even for typically developing youngsters. Within ABA, attention has been given to identifying related skills that might predict readiness for understanding humor. For example, Weiss and Harris (2001) have suggested that it might help to lay a foundation for identifying silliness and absurdity, and for tuning in to subtlety and nuance (see Table 4.9).

Table 4.9
Possible Foundations for Teaching Humor

ITEMS WITH MISSING PARTS
A house without a roof
A bike without a wheel

MISPLACED ITEMS
A shoe on a child's head
A car with a sail

ILLOGICAL ITEMS
Coloring with a fork
Wearing a snowsuit in the summer

ABSURD ITEMS
A baby driving a car
A dog on roller skates

It is helpful when teaching humor to make the teaching context as natural as possible. Weiss and Harris (2001) recommend that a second instructor help the child respond appropriately to jokes. (This prevents the joke teller from having to step out of role to assist the learner in how to respond.) A second instructor can also highlight the aspects of a joke that make it particularly funny (such as in a play on words).

Nonverbal communication. Another area in which many students with HFA/AS struggle is identifying and interpreting nonverbal communication. Even at very young ages, children communicate a great deal without using words. Body language, facial expression, and gestures all are used to let others know how we feel.

Students on the spectrum may fail to understand what others are communicating when it is not accompanied by words. This deficit is common, and it has major social consequences. It is usually helpful to teach some of this content very directly to ensure that the student gets adequate and clear exposure to the concept.

JOSÉ'S shadow (i.e., instructional assistant available to provide prompting/redirection and reinforcement as needed in an inclusive educational environment; see also Chapter 3) made a list of all of the nonverbal teacher signals and peer behaviors she observed in a week at school. She then taught José exactly what they meant. She said, "Sometimes the teacher does this," and then she would engage in the target behavior (such as raising hand to lips). What does it mean? What should you do when you see it?" They would rehearse the action in response to the cue and label it (for informational purposes). In this way, she introduced the content (i.e., it means, "be quiet") and provided opportunities to practice the response. She also collected data on how often José responded to these cues (with and without her help) to track whether the skill was transferring to the natural environment.

A combination of direct instruction, behavioral rehearsal, and generalization training can be very successful in helping children with HFA/AS to comprehend and respond to nonverbal communications.

Perspective taking. Children with ASD have difficulty standing in the shoes of another person, and comprehending what another person's experience might be. Such "mindblindness" has been described as being blind to certain aspects of social and emotional experience, such as others' thoughts, beliefs, desires, and intentions (Baron-Cohen, 1997). Individuals with deficits in this area lack the intuitive understanding of mental states, and fail to notice or label such states in themselves and in others (Hill & Frith, 2003). Attributing mental states to others is a critical skill for making social sense of the world (Baron-Cohen, 1997).

Examples of skills requiring perspective taking include:

- Compassion (understanding sadness, disappointment of others)

- Comforting (understanding desire of others for comfort)

- Understanding lying (comprehending personal gain)

- Inquiring about how others feel about something (understanding feelings are individual)

A large body of literature documents the deficits that children with ASD exhibit in this area. For example, children have been shown to have difficulty in false belief tasks (i.e., tasks in which they need to predict the behavior of another person who is missing important information, such as the fact that an object has been moved from its location). Individuals with ASD also have trouble understanding irony, pretense, and deception (Hill & Frith, 2003). Further, they also have difficulty assessing the actions and motives of characters in stories (e.g., Dewey, 1991; Happé, 1994; Happé et al., 1996).

Such deficits impair the ability to function successfully in social contexts. For example, it makes it difficult to assess the intent of another person, making children vulnerable to teasing and to bullying. Children with HFA/AS are already likely targets for teasing, given their often atypical style of socialization (e. g., lurking near others, answering in noncontextual ways, initiating in ways that others find confusing or odd), their unusual interests, and their social naiveté. Problems in social understanding may make it very difficult to understand what is happening (e.g., Ozonoff, Dawson, & McPartland, 2002).

The question is whether such deficits are remediable. Can we teach perspective-taking skills in a meaningful way? If we teach such skills, will they transfer to real-life situations? Much work needs to be done in teaching these skills and in assessing how well such instruction prepares learners for social situations requiring the ability to understand someone else's point of view.

Weiss and Harris (2001) have outlined some preliminary skills to target in the development of perspective taking (see Table 4.10). For example, they suggest making the initial stages of perspective training very concrete, focusing on what objects individuals can see in their visual field.

Table 4.10
Ways to Train Perspective Taking

VISUAL FIELD EXERCISES
Seat two dolls next to each other, but facing in opposite directions. In front of one doll, there is a ball and a puzzle. In front of the other doll, there is a duck and a car. Ask the children whether the doll facing the ball can see the ball, and then whether she can see the duck. The same questions may be asked about the second doll. This activity can be expanded into demonstrations that include the child.

Call attention to how an object is being used. (It is really a bowl, but she is pretending it is a hat.)

FOCUSING ON THE ABILITY TO PERCEIVE VS. THE INABILITY TO PERCEIVE SOMETHING
Focus on helping your child to answer when he or she can and cannot see certain objects. Vary the ability to see by placing objects in containers, behind curtains, etc. Start by having the children enter the room after you have hidden the object. Later, have them watch you hide the object, and target their ability to answer whether they can see it (in actuality).

FOCUSING ON SOMETHING'S APPEARANCE (VS. ITS REALITY)
Use a variety of magnets, pens, and erasers made to appear to be something else. Have the child answer what it looks like vs. what it truly is.

LOGICAL VS. ILLOGICAL PLACEMENT OF OBJECTS
Help the child learn to identify what people predict is inside different boxes (i.e., people will expect there to be raisins in a raisin box and crackers in a cracker box). Vary what is actually placed in the containers. Help the children to understand what other people (who do not know about the shuffling of objects) will predict to be inside the boxes.

ORIENTING FIGURES APPROPRIATELY
Bridge into social perspective taking by lining up or arranging characters with proper orientation to teacher and peers for various activities (going to recess, circle time). Have the child correct misorientations.

UTILITY OF GAZE
Create games to help children understand how important eye contact is. You may ask them to figure out which candy you want the most by watching which one you look at. You can make this activity more fun by having them watch your eyes for a clue as to where you have hidden a treat for both of you (i.e., a favorite snack or movie).

Table 4.10 (cont.)

DIFFERENTIAL EXPERIENCE
Set up situations to ask questions about experiences in which the child's experience differs from yours. For example, teachers can show photos from their own summer vacation and ask the children if they think they would have fun there. Similarly, photos or stories from the child's life can be used to differentiate an instructor's experience (i.e., the instructor was not present; it was not a shared experience).

A wide variety of everyday examples can be used in this exercise, including trips to the doctor or dentist, attending a birthday party, getting a haircut, going to the zoo, riding a Ferris wheel, etc. The goal is to help the child learn that people have different experiences and that the ability to answer a question about an event is based on whether you participated in it.

PERSPECTIVE-TAKING GAME
This is a variation of a classic assessment for perspective-taking ability. Hide an object in the room. Ask someone to leave the room. Together with the child, move the object from the first hidden location to a second hidden location. Ask the friend to return to the room. Help the target student learn to predict what the person will say about where the object is hidden. (Most individuals with ASD will assume that the person who exited will have the new information about the second location, when in fact the person was not present when the object was moved.) The goal of this activity is to help the learner understand that experience is not universal. People who have different information and experiences answer questions and approach situations differently.

Joint attention. Joint attention has been described as coordinating attention to an event or an object with another individual, sharing interest, and demonstrating an understanding that the partner is sharing the same experience (Schertz & Odom, 2004). It essentially involves shared experience. Common examples from typical development include toddlers pointing out objects such as an airplane in the sky, looking to see that their caretaker sees the plane, too. Joint attention has been defined narrowly, such as gazing where someone else is gazing (Butterworth,

1991), and broadly, as behaviors utilized in "opening or maintaining a communicative channel with the partner" (Sigman & Kasari, 1995, p. 190). Deficits in joint attention are prominent among individuals with ASD (Kasari, Sigman, Mundy, & Yirmiya, 1990; Levy & Dawson, 1992; Mundy, Sigman, & Kasari, 1990).

One central question within ABA is whether joint attention skills can be taught, and whether such skills generalize into natural contexts. Encouraging research has demonstrated that joint attention skills can be increased (e.g., Baker, 2000; Pierce & Schreibman, 1995; Whalen & Schreibman, 2003; Zercher, Hunt, Schuler, & Webster, 2001). Clinicians are increasingly trying to build social attention, sharing of experience, and attention to nonverbal communication in children with HFA/AS.

Recently, a number of clinicians from varying theoretical perspectives have focused attention on the development of joint attention and perspective taking. For example, relationship development intervention (RDI) uses "relationship coaching" to guide children into the social world (Gutstein & Sheely, 2002). Gutstein (2000) has described various stages of experience sharing (see Table 4.11) that are extremely important in terms of emotional development and social attachment.

Table 4.11
Levels and Stages of Experience Sharing

Tuning In (birth)
    Includes observing the facial reactions of adults and sharing excitement

Learning to Dance (6 months)
    Includes synchronizing actions with a partner (working together)

Improvising and Co-Creating (12 months)
    Includes adding novelty into activities (improvisation) and combining sequences of actions (more elaborate and fluid interaction)

Sharing Outside Worlds (18 months)
    Includes perception sharing (joint attention: looking at the same thing) and perspective taking (noticing that we may be experiencing different things)

Discovering Inside Worlds (30 months)
    Includes attention to feelings (attention to thoughts, feelings, ideas)

Binding Selves to Others (48 months)
    Includes defining self in terms of similarities to and differences from others and having a sense of group membership

From *Autism Aspergers: Solving the Relationship Puzzle* by S. E. Gutstein (pp. 12-13), 2000, Arlington, TX: Future Horizons. Used with permission.

While there is a lack of data on the effectiveness of this approach, the authors cite several activities that are compatible with other interventions (including ABA), including the following.

- Building gaze shifting from one person to another through the use of a "swing and fly" procedure (Gutstein & Sheely, 2002)

In this activity, the child moves between two coaches. The coaches use pausing to build anticipation and encourage the child to look at them in an alternating manner, in order to be swung repeatedly on a beanbag chair.

- Building interest in eye contact by playing a game

The child is asked to find a hidden object, but is given only the clue of watching the coach's face. The coach looks at the area where the hidden object is located. In this way, the child learns to watch for what a play/conversational partner is looking at. Extensions of this game can include reversing roles and using frowns and smiles as nonverbal feedback (about how close the child is to getting the correct location).

Later stages of instruction within RDI target a variety of other socially relevant behaviors, including understanding interpersonal space and telling jokes. Activities suggested by Gutstein and Sheely (2002) provide a nice supplement to any other work you may be doing in these areas.

In their jokes activity section, Gutstein and Sheely (2002) suggest working with two children as a joke-telling team, fist helping each one to take the roles of teller and straight man, and then evolving into a team of joke tellers (with an audience). Aspects of joke telling that are emphasized as being important include timing (e.g., waiting until the straight man has communicated that he doesn't know the answer before delivering the punch line) and sharing the laughter with the joke partner.

Social Communication Training

Social language (language that is used to get someone's attention or to respond to someone) is a substantial challenge for many learners on the spectrum. Thus, students with HFA/AS often find themselves in social circumstances unsure of how to respond or how to initiate.

Moore (2002) described the use of *"I can say" cards*. These cards give students with HFA/AS rules about options for responding in given scenarios. While they are developed for students in elementary school, they may be adapted for younger learners. The cards focus on the following eight skills:

1. Accepting/rejecting an object or invitation
2. Asking a friend to play
3. Joining a game
4. Dealing with rejection from an individual
5. Dealing with rejection from a group
6. Requesting assistance
7. Offering assistance
8. Expressing opinions

Moore describes using the cards to help students identify when to use these skills/scripts. She suggests combining role-playing rehearsal with the activity to help children practice a given skill. She also suggests the use of rewards during role-play activities and in spontaneous situations where the learner applies the social language rules. An extension of the strategy is to include information on what *not* to say. In this way, the learner can be sensitized to not say things others might find insensitive or annoying.

Social language groups are another excellent way to target social deficits. Moore (2002) describes the use of such groups by Sally Bligh. The focus of these groups is to increase peer communication. Strategies include scripting, game playing, exploring special interests, positive reinforcement, modeling, and role-playing, which are described below. An example scripting is presented in Table 4.12.

Table 4.12
Sample Scripting Situation

Scripting: In this intervention, the adult provides the child with the exact words he or she should say. It is used when the child does not know what to say in a social situation.

- "Can I play, too?"
- "Please give me back my ball."
- "I want a turn."

Game playing: This is used to encourage verbal interchange. Activities selected must require interaction.

Exploring special interests: The child's special interest is used to motivate and encourage participation and interaction.

Positive reinforcement: Concrete and visible rewards are used to reinforce desirable social behavior.

- Stickers
- Points

Modeling: The facilitator demonstrates appropriate behaviors to the observing group.

Role-playing: Practicing and rehearsing of social situations is used to further hone skills. Videotaping is also often used to allow for later review.

In creating a social language group, attention is paid to the communication levels of the children, the number of kids in the group, the activities or games targeted, and the reward system to be used. Furthermore, specific activities are selected and skills are targeted for learners at different language levels. For example, for a child who mostly interacts by giving commands, the rule might be talk to each other in a way to make friends. Reciprocity would be emphasized and reinforced throughout all activities.

Social Stories™, developed by Carol Gray (1993, 1994), focus on helping individuals on the autism spectrum to comprehend social circumstances. Social Stories™ may also be used to assist learners in understanding the perspectives of others. Examples include helping learners to understand the pride others will feel for them when they succeed, the sadness or hurt others feel when they are the victims of aggression, and the confusion peers might feel when their social overtures are ignored.

Using perspective statements provides information on the feelings of others, and provides a rationale for some of the directive statements contained within Social Stories™. Gray recommends a ratio of 1 to 2:5 directive to other statements. In other words, the majority of statements are descriptive (telling about the situation) or perspective (conveying the feelings of others). A small percentage of the statements actually directly instructs the person about what to do. See examples in Figure 4.2.

Many social circumstances present themselves differently on each occasion, and this variability confuses many on the autism spectrum. Also, many social skills involve doing several things at the same time, depending on the context. For example, even

Daniel uses an inside voice ...

Hi, my name is Daniel.
(Descriptive Statement)

I like to talk.
(Descriptive Statement)

But people cannot hear me when I talk.
(Perspective Statement)

My friend's inside voice is not too
soft and not too loud.
(Descriptive Statement)

When I talk, I will: 1. Pick up my head.
(Directive Statement)

When I talk, I will: 2. Look at who
I am talking to.
(Directive Statement)

When I talk, I will: 3. Talk louder.
(Directive Statement)

Then, everyone will know what I am saying!!
(Perspective Statement)

Figure 4.2. Examples of sentence types in Social Stories™.

a task as concrete as lining up can be dismally confusing to a young child with HFA/AS. The child may be first on line, last on line, behind Joey, or behind Abigail. This variability is normal for this event, and we cannot predict exactly how the situation will unfold each time it arises.

We need to prepare learners for the multiplicity of potential circumstances. While it is not possible to predict every single circumstance that may be encountered, we want to prepare learners for more than one eventuality. Social Stories™ can be written to address this issue, with information on multiple possible variations in experience or reaction. (For example, in lining up for recess, the story can be written to say. "I might be first on line. I might be last on line. I might be behind Rebecca. I might be behind Colleen.")

Social Stories™ have also been used to target behavioral challenges or address fear situations. In these circumstances, it is especially important to review the story as a regular part of the school day (and not solely in preparation for or a review of a challenging moment).

In general, it is helpful to use pictures to further highlight the salient messages of the story (Kutter, Myles, & Carlson, 1998; Sansoti, Powell-Smith, & Kincaid, 2004). Some students respond best to the use of photographs, making the connection to their circumstances even more concrete. It is also often helpful to write the story in the first person. Figure 4.3 is an example of a Social Story™.

Charlie's Story

My name is Charlie. I am 4 years old.

I am a big boy now. I can do many things.

I can go to school on the school bus all by myself.

I can go to the bathroom all by myself.

I can make cookies and decorate them with sprinkles.

I love to play with my friends.

We like to run and tickle each other and fall down on the ground.

Sometimes my friends don't like it when I tickle too much. They tell me to stop.

When someone says stop, I need to listen. They may say "stop," "no more," or "leave me alone."

When my friends tell me to stop, I can walk away, play a new game, or find another friend and play.

When I remember to be a big boy and use quiet hands with my friends, I can use my hands for fun in karate.

Figure 4.3. Sample Social Story™.

Myles and Southwick (2005) suggested using Social Stories™ in a structured, data-based way, including taking baseline and intervention data and programming for generalization and maintenance. These are suggestions that are commonly used when Social Stories™ are used as part of behaviorally oriented intervention or ABA.

Problem-Solving Training

Problem-solving training has received increased attention in recent years within behavior therapy and across many populations of learners (e.g., Shure, 1992). The steps of such procedures usually involve:

1. Identification of the problem

2. Generation of alternative solutions

3. Anticipating consequences of solutions

4. Choosing the best option

5. Evaluating the choice

There are many advantages to problem-solving strategy training. For example, it helps learners identify clearly what the social problem is and what options are available as a response. Many learners have difficulty explicitly articulating a social problem, and many more have difficulty perceiving that there may be dozens of potential responses.

Using a protocol helps children to perceive multiple options for reacting, and this can reduce impulsive responding. Imagining what would happen if different paths are taken is also helpful, as it helps make connections between behaviors and consequences (e.g., if I hit back, I will get in trouble; if I tell the teacher, she will help resolve the problem).

The following illustrates the use of a problem-solving strategy.

Joey was lined up to go out for recess, and his friend pushed him.

Problem: *Joey got pushed by his friend.*

Options and consequences:

Options	Consequences
Pushing back	*Likely both get in trouble*
Screaming to stop	*May get in trouble*
Tell the teacher	*Teacher will help resolve it*
Ask friend to stop	*Friend may or may not stop*

The SOCCSS (Situation, Options, Consequences, Choices, Strategies, & Simulation) procedure was developed by Jan Roosa for individuals with ASD, and is designed to focus on social problems either before or after they occur (Myles & Southwick, 2005). As illustrated in Table 4.13, the steps of this procedure are similar to the steps involved in other problem-solving training approaches, especially those within a behavioral framework. Table 4.14 is a blank SOCCSS worksheet.

Table 4.13
SOCCSS Strategy

Situation: Answering Wh-questions about the incident
Options: Brainstorming options for behavioral reaction
Consequences: Identifying a likely outcome for each option
Choices: Choosing an option
Strategies: Developing a plan of action for the chosen option
Simulation: Practicing through imagery, discussion, writing, or role-playing
    Example:
    Lauren is on the playground. She is playing with a ball. Joey comes
    up to her and grabs the ball away. Lauren yells. The teacher comes
    over to see what is happening.

Situation: Answering Wh-questions about the incident
    Joey takes a ball from Lauren.

Options: Brainstorming options for behavioral reaction
    Give the ball to Joey
    Ask Joey to give it back
    Pull Joey's hair
    Hit Joey
    Tell the teacher

Consequences: Identifying a likely outcome for each option
    Lauren feels sad, cries
    Joey keeps the ball
    Joey cries & tells the teacher. Lauren (& Joey) get in trouble
    Joey cries and tells the teacher. Lauren (& Joey) get in trouble
    The teacher makes Joey give the ball back

Choices: Choosing an option
    Tell the teacher

Strategies: Developing a plan of action for the chosen option
    Discuss how to do it

Simulation: Practice through imagery, discussion, writing, or role-playing
    Role-play with dolls, discuss the scenario, review concept again with
    slightly changed content to ensure generalization.

Table 4.14
SOCCSS Worksheet

Situation	
Who	When
What	Why

Options	Consequences	Choices

Strategy – Plan of Action

Simulation	Select One
1. Find a quiet place, sit back and imagine how your Situation would work (or not work) based on the various Options and Consequences.	
2. Talk with a peer, staff, or other person about your plan of action.	
3. Write down on paper what may happen in your Situation based on your Options and Consequences.	
4. Practice your Options with one or more people using behavior rehearsal. Start simple and easy for learning. Only make it difficult to test the learning.	
5. _____	

Simulation Outcomes

Followup

From Asperger Syndrome and Difficult Moments – Practical Solutions for Tantrums, Rage, and Meltdowns (pp. 115-116), by B. S. Myles and J. Southwick, 2005, Shawnee Mission, KS: Autism Asperger Publishing Company. Created by Myles, 1998, from the work of Roosa, J. B. (1995). *Men on the move: Competence and cooperation "Conflict resolution and beyond."* Kansas City, MO: Author. Reprinted with permission.

Another good source for information on problem solving is *The Way to A* (Manasco, 2006), which provides graphics for choosing a course of action when a problem occurs. It reviews the negative effects of a poor choice, including the behavioral outburst, the negative feelings, and the social consequences. It also reviews better choices. Color and letter coding is used to facilitate appropriate choice making, providing additional visual cues. Figure 4.4 illustrates (unfortunately, without the use of the prominent colors red and green), the consequences of good and poor choices. The simple and visual nature of this graph is well suited for use with young children.

In addition, *The Incredible 5-Point Scale* (Buron & Curtis, 2003) is an excellent tool for helping learners to track their degree of emotional upset and to eventually monitor when they are climbing the scale of agitation. In this way, they may learn to cue into feelings of upset prior to a full-blown meltdown. Figure 4.5 shows an example of a 5-point scale used to monitor stress.

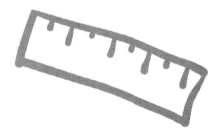

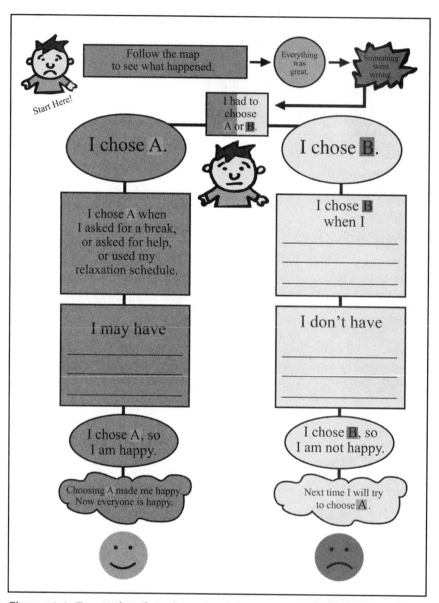

Figure 4.4. Example of problem-solving approach.

From Manasco, H. (2006). *The Way to A: Empowering Children with Autism Spectrum and Other Neurological Disorders to Monitor and Replace Aggression and Tantrum Behavior* (p. 17). Shawnee Mission, KS: Autism Asperger Publishing Company. Used with permission.

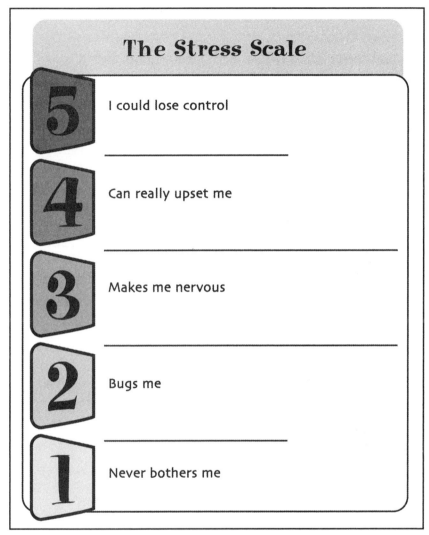

Figure 4.5. Stress Scale.

From Buron, K. D., & Curtis, M. (2006). *The Incredible 5-Point Scale – Assisting Students with Autism Spectrum Disorders in Understanding Social Interactions and Controlling Their Emotional Responses* (p. 65). Shawnee Mission, KS: Autism Asperger Publishing Company. Used with permission.

Relaxation is also increasingly being used as a problem-solving approach to help reduce the feelings of anxiety that are so common among children with HFA/AS. Even young children can learn such simple strategies as the one depicted in Figure 4.6.

1. Take three long breaths.
2. Stretch your arms up over your head, down and up again.
3. Rub your hands together and count to 3.
4. Rub your thighs and count to 3.
5. Take another long breath.

Figure 4.6. My calming sequence.

From Buron, K. D. (2006). *When My Worries Get Too Big! A Relaxation Book for Children Who Live with Anxiety* (p. 9). Shawnee Mission, KS: Autism Asperger Publishing Company. Used with permission.

Whatever protocol is implemented, problem-solving training should focus on identifying options and anticipating consequences. If behavioral rehearsal strategies can be used and multiple learning modalities are involved, the transfer of skills to the natural environment is likely to increase.

Summary

Intervention for young children with HFA/AS is complex and multifaceted. The sensory issues and characteristics of many of these learners have led to sensory integration as a common approach to intervention. Despite many anecdotal reports of the positive impact of this type of intervention, rigorous empirical support is lacking. However, SI approaches may be combined with many other interventions. For example, sensory needs can be evaluated in a functional assessment, and sensory experiences can be provided on a schedule to prevent escalation of behavior. Furthermore, sensory experiences can be provided as reinforcement for appropriate behavior. Finally, data may also be collected on the utility and effects of SI treatment on any individual learner. In this way, the merits of the approach can be validated and the need for alteration of the approach can be assessed.

The intervention with the strongest empirical support is applied behavior analysis. ABA has evolved over time, and now incorporates many naturalistic strategies in addition to formal teaching methods. Although originally used with individuals on the severe end of the autism spectrum, ABA strategies have relevance for individuals who are higher functioning. The social deficits in autism remain the hardest to address, but progress has been made in targeting these skills deficits in social initiation, social responsiveness, and social comprehension. Many of the strategies that can be successful in remediating these deficits are either ABA strategies or can easily be incorporated into an ABA approach. These include Social Stories™, rule cards, and problem-solving approaches.

Many other strategies used to address social deficits overlap with those covered in the ABA section. For example, relationship development intervention targets many of the deficits addressed within ABA through activities that can be incorporated into other instructional efforts. Social communication approaches and social problem-solving approaches are very helpful in reducing challenging behaviors and in building social skills.

Chapter 5

TEAMWORK

Serving young children with HFA/AS requires a coordinated effort by many professionals and the child's family and caregivers. The importance of teamwork in achieving goals cannot be overstated. Communication between parents and professionals is the first ingredient in creating an effective and functional team. Teams that are effective are able to manage conflict and differing opinions, compromise, see the viewpoints of other team members, and celebrate successes. Professionals must also find a way to work collaboratively with one another, respecting the individual expertise of each professional and agreeing on priorities and approaches. This chapter will present an overview of ways in which collaboration may be enhanced.

Communication Between Parents and Professionals

Communication between parents and professionals is the foundation on which effective home-school collaboration is built. When parents and professionals work together effectively, there are major benefits for the student. Furthermore, in the context of parent-professional partnership, family members who are full members of the team (who participate in meetings and goal development, and who feel understood and valued by the team) feel empowered or able to make an impact in their child's education (Rosenkoetter, Hains, & Fowler, 1994).

It is essential to have open communication between all members of the team, and especially for young children, the link between parents and professionals may be the most crucial. For young children, the majority of their social experiences have occurred in their homes with their families. Families, therefore, have a wealth of information that is essential in planning successful school experiences.

By the same token, parents need to be fully informed of major events that happen in the course of a child's experience. This includes daily successes, significant struggles, and social connections. Many teachers or teams use a daily notebook that goes back and forth between home and school, in which they can record comments on the day, notes on assignments for the evening, upcoming information such as changes in schedule or routine (e.g., Moore, 2002), and so on.

Other teachers and teams find it helpful to use a structured note that highlights several issues on a daily basis. The sample home-school note in Figure 5.1 includes areas for commenting about social interactions, learning center performance, noteworthy positive accomplishments, as well as noteworthy challenges. There are also sections for significant events or activities that occurred during the day.

Home-School Note ___/___/___	
Social Interactions	**Significant Class Events or Activities That Student May Discuss at Home**
Learning Center Performance	
Noteworthy Positive Accomplishments	**Upcoming Lessons**
Noteworthy Challenges	
Other Comments	

Figure 5.1. Sample home-school notes.

Completed Home-School Note Home-School Note __10_/__22_/__06_	
Social Interactions Responded to Kira's and Kaitlin's greetings!! Asked Bobby to (join) building blocks	**Significant Class Events or Activities That Student May Discuss at Home** Leaf rubbing (fall theme) "Five Little Pumpkins" song
Learning Center Performance Great counting ghosts and witches, worked on 1 to 5	
Noteworthy Positive Accomplishments Walked to water fountain without touching the wall (hands in pockets) Stayed in circle time for the whole time Shared pretzels with Alex at snack	**Upcoming Lessons** Pumpkin patch trip on Friday "Who Scared the Moon?" book
Noteworthy Challenges Difficulty cleaning up after blocks (needed multiple reminders and physical prompts) Still forgetting to close bathroom door	
Other Comments	

Figure 5.1. Sample home-school notes. (cont.)

This type of communication can serve as a springboard for parents to talk with their child about his day. This is a good strategy to use with learners who have difficulty reporting events of the day, or who answer questions very simply and without elaboration. That is, the parent can use the information provided to create a more lengthy interaction about the day. Finally, the note includes a section for information on upcoming lessons. This can be very helpful in priming or preparing students for a new theme, book, or topic.

Many teachers and families also find it helpful to communicate at times via email or by phone, depending on the circumstances that arise. It is helpful if the teacher and parent can agree on how they will communicate when they need to communicate quickly. The teacher may prefer to call at a certain time, or to be emailed. Letting a parent know these preferences can make for much more effective (and less frustrating) communication for all.

Professionals must be positive and proactive in dealing with families. The following strategies can reduce the likelihood of misunderstanding and foster respect and trust.

Accentuate the Positive

Many parents of children with special needs have been subject to litanies of complaints. Even a young child may have a history of "complaints" or concerns from educators. No child demonstrates only problem behavior. Educators must remember to emphasize the positive in what the child is doing, demonstrating, and learning. There is a tendency to overlook those aspects of a child's functioning, or to perceive them as irrelevant. However, sharing the positives balances the focus on challenges, and provides parents with a fuller view of the child.

MR. AND MRS. MARTIN had heard it all about Luke. They had heard about his oppositionality, his incorrigibility, and his lack of attention. Whenever they were contacted by a teacher or attended a parent-teacher conference during his preschool years, most or all of the discussion seemed to center on his deficits and on the difficulties he posed to teaching staff.

When Luke entered kindergarten, they feared the worst. So they were pleasantly surprised at Back to School Night when the teacher shared how impressed she was with Luke's imagination, with his art-work, and with his reading. They also discussed the challenges, but the balance was greatly appreciated.

Be Ready with Solutions When Bringing up Problems or Concerns

It is a good idea to have a solution in mind (or preferably, several possibilities) when raising a concern. In this way, the discussion rather immediately becomes focused on solving the problem.

When MRS. GREEVY approached Jessica's parents about her contin-ued difficulties in circle time, she had a plan in mind. She asked their permission for Jessica to join the circle for just the last 5 minutes. When Jessica could be successful with that length of time, she would extend it further. She told them that she wanted Jessica to join the end of the circle rather than the beginning, because she thought Jessica would enjoy transitioning from circle with the whole group to snack (a highly preferred activity). The Greevy family appreciated the thought and in-tent of the plan, and agreed to it. The focus of the conversation was on the teacher's optimism about implementing the plan.

Respect Parents' Perspective, Information, History, and Opinions

Parents are experts about their children, and there is no substitute for their history and long-term perspective on their child's characteristics and needs. Respecting their opinions is appropriate and essential, and can save countless hours of trial-and-error, frustration, and miscommunication.

MRS. WINSLOW appreciated that her team listened to her perspective regarding Brandon's behaviors. She felt that he had tremendous sensitivity to sound, dating back from early infancy, and that he could not be made to endure fire drills. She begged the team to come up with an alternative that would allow him to avoid, and perhaps eventually to quickly escape, the sound. She gave many examples of her son's sensory hypersensitivity and of unsuccessful attempts to make him overcome them. The team developed a plan to allow him to "take a walk" outside just prior to the bell going off, as a first step. They also worked on a plan to systematically and gradually desensitize him to the fire drill noise by using a recorded sample of the fire alarm, and gradually increasing his tolerance for the volume of the sound as well as for the duration of the alarm. Other adjustments included giving Brandon a way to modulate the sound (headphones) and allowing him to leave with his aide immediately (vs. having to wait for the rest of the class to exit).

Be Honest with Parents About Your Professional Limitations and About When More/Other Expertise Is Needed

Educators expect themselves to have all the answers. However, at times, our expertise falls short. For example, a child may present with a feeding disorder that requires an expert with specialized training in that area, or a child's behavior problem may be more complex than any previously encountered by the team, and may not be responding to their best efforts. It is a sign of strength, not of weakness, to indicate a need for outside expertise in extraordinary circumstances. Parents respect professionals for their honesty and directness.

MAUREEN'S food rigidities started escalating, which alarmed the staff. All the usual procedures they employed to increase variability of foods accepted had failed. There were days at school when Maureen ate and drank nothing. They began to see behavioral regression. They approached Maureen's parents and requested that they seek an outside evaluation and consultation from a feeding disorders specialist. Maureen's parents respected the team's message, and agreed that they needed an expert to help them address a problem that none of them could solve.

Realize There Will Be Differences of Opinion and Some Awkward Moments

Both parenting and educating are highly complex endeavors that are often surrounded by strong emotions and strong opinions. Inevitably, there will be times when parents and professionals disagree. This is not a catastrophe. It is the management of conflict, not the avoidance of conflict, that characterizes effective collaboration.

ADAM'S mother was disappointed when she realized how far apart she was from Adam's teacher about how to address his social deficits. She wanted the team to begin working on perspective-taking and problem-solving skills, but the teacher wanted to work on much more basic skills in the social realm, including identification of emotions and cause-effect relationships. They worked through the conflict, real-

izing that they shared the same vision and the same ultimate outcomes and that it was more a matter of timeframes and prerequisite skills. They were able to work out and compromise on goals that were realistic, achievable, and focused on the long-term acquisition of the complex social skills Adam needed to acquire.

Contain Your Emotions When Controversy Arises

It is never a good idea to react intensely and emotionally in the moment. When we react in the moment, we may say things that we later regret.

It is a good strategy to monitor your reactions, recognize when emotions are strong, and let some time pass before you address the situation. After having time to reflect and think through the situation, convey your concerns. In many cases, the communication you engage in at those times will be clearer and calmer, and less likely to further fuel the debate.

When MRS. BURKE was told of the bullying her son had endured at school, she went ballistic. It activated every parental fiber of her being, and she was enraged at staff for not protecting him adequately. She said little at the moment she found out, fearing she would fall apart, and decided to address it with staff the next day. When she did, she was able to calmly articulate her disappointment, as well as her hopes for better management of the situation. Further, she was calm enough to listen intently when staff presented their bullying prevention plan, a classwide initiative to target the behavior on a global scale. She was pleased that the intervention would be broader than just her son, and was optimistic that it would have the desired impact.

Address Difficulties and Propose a Solution

When a problem arises between parents and professionals, it is best to directly address it (and not to ignore it). Whenever possible, propose a solution along with the presenting issue. For example, if a parent is upset because the teacher is too busy to send home sufficient information in advance of lessons, it may be a good idea if the parent offers to be a classroom volunteer once a week and to help prepare materials.

MRS. SWEENEY, a parent, was calling the teacher several times a day, often during class time when it was difficult for the teacher to get to the phone or be fully available to converse. Explaining that she was not able to accept calls randomly throughout the day, the teacher offered a plan, proposing that they speak daily either at 2:45 p.m. or twice a week at 8:15 a.m. The mother chose to speak twice a week at 8:15 a.m. Eventually, they reduced the frequency to a weekly call, and then to every other week.

Engage in Active Listening

This may seem obvious, but it is easier said than done. Active listening involves giving the other party a chance to fully express his or her point of view. It is often helpful to paraphrase what the other person has said, in an effort to convey that you have heard what was said. Just being heard and understood fosters a feeling of cooperation and camaraderie.

MS. POWELL, Erin's teacher, found it difficult to listen to Erin's mother's perspective on why it was impossible for her to get Erin to school on time. In many ways, she just seemed full of excuses. But one day she promised herself she would listen more actively to her. Taking a proactive step made her feel less irritated. More important, by listening attentively, she learned that Erin's mother was under tremendous strain and that the morning routine was completely unmanageable for the whole family. She felt empathy toward the woman, and recognized that her helplessness was not laziness or a lack of cooperation. Together, they were able to more effectively dialogue about the issues, and create a plan for extra supports at home in the morning on a short-term basis to make things go more smoothly.

Reinforce and Shape Desirable Behavior

It is always a good idea to notice when others are engaging in desirable behavior. We emphasize this in working with our students, but sometimes forget to extend it to our other interactions! Notes and comments of appreciation go a long way toward building effective teaming.

MEGAN'S MOTHER was delighted when she saw that the list of books to be read at reading circle were coming home at the beginning of each month for the whole month. It gave her a chance to collect them and integrate them into time at home. To express her appreciation, she made sure to send the teacher a thank-you note, indicating how much easier it made it for her to link the efforts at home and school.

Gather Information Systematically, Especially When There Is a Difference of Opinion

When a difference of opinion is substantial, it is sometimes advisable to turn to an objective source of information. Thus, the team has facts, including pros and cons, on which to base a decision.

MRS. ROSCO insists that her child, Braeden, needs 10 minutes of exercise every hour to keep him from becoming too overactive and to facilitate his paying attention. She has seen over the years how regular activity helps him to focus, but staff members are concerned about how that would fit into the schedule and whether it is truly necessary. After reaching a stalemate, a member of the team suggests that they collect some data on the benefits of exercising. They decide to compare Braeden's activity and attention on days in which there is access to regular exercise versus days in which there is not access to regular exercise. In this way, the team would have an objective index of the importance of the strategy to help guide their decision. Everyone agrees on the merits of this plan, and they formulate a systematic examination of the impact of exercise.

Table 5.1
Being Professional with Parents: Top 10 List

1. Accentuate the positive

2. Be ready with solutions when you bring up problems or concerns for discussion

3. Respect the parent's perspective, information, history, and opinions

4. Be honest with parents about your professional limitations and about when more expertise is needed

5. Realize that there will be differences of opinion and awkward moments

6. Contain your emotion when controversy arises

7. Address difficulties in interactions and propose a solution

8. Engage in active listening

9. Reinforce and shape desirable behavior of other adults!

10. Gather more information systematically, especially when there is a difference of opinion

---

Communication Between Teacher and Student

It is also important to have a strong and direct communicative link between the teacher and the student. While this is built and fostered every day during myriad interactions, it is a good idea to add in other bond-building activities. One way is to arrange for the student to occasionally have lunch with the teacher, or with the teacher and a small group of peers (Moore, 2002). This can create an informal context for building rapport, for checking in with the student, and for fostering a social connection. It is an opportunity for more teacher-student contact and/or for peer integration. It is often very difficult for teachers to find time to spend with a student 1:1, and this forum affords them a chance to connect with them person to person. They might use the opportunity to discuss some of the student's special interests or to plan special projects that would be very interesting and reinforcing to the student. If the time is used to foster social connections among a small group of peers, it can be structured to facilitate conversation, play, and group participation skills.

Communication Within the Team

All efforts will be for naught if team members fail to work effectively together. Creating a functional team is essential to success. Team members of children with HFA/AS typically include the parents, the teacher, paraprofessionals involved with the child, professionals delivering ancillary services such as speech, occupational and physical therapists, a behavior analyst or specialist, and supervisors or administrators. Many of these same individuals are present in teams for young children as well, and the team foci are generally on family involvement, home-relevant skills, and collaboration between all parties to ensure success.

Effective groups demonstrate several characteristics (Amason, Thompson, Hochwarter, & Harrison, 1995). First of all, they are focused. Second, they are creative. They approach solutions to problems from different and novel perspectives. Third, they use open communication. Lastly, they integrate all members.

These are very important dimensions of effective teamwork within the context of educational planning. Being focused helps the team to retain its focus on the student and his/her goals. Agreement on the goals of the team is, in fact, an essential prerequisite to successful teamwork; it is only possible to work together once the objectives have been agreed upon (Amason et al., 1995; Moore, 2002).

Approaching solutions from different and novel perspectives is one of the great potential assets of a team; each member has a unique expertise and perspective, allowing for divergent perspectives and approaches. Given the complexity and diversity of issues faced by students with HFA/AS, such rich diversity within a team is extraordinarily useful. The integration of all team members is also essential in this context. The student, the parent, and each professional should be represented, respected, and heard. It is the only way to ensure comprehensive assessment of student needs and thorough program planning. Table 5.2 lists the major characteristics of effective teams.

Table 5.2 *Characteristics of Effective Teams*
1. Agreed-upon, consistent focus
2. Creativity
3. Open communication

HARRISON was a very bright preschooler. He was exceptionally skilled in using the computer and could figure out almost anything without direct instruction. Some members of his team saw the computer as a great asset, as a special skill and an area in which his abilities exceeded those of his peers. Other members of the team hated the computer, wanting to remove it from the room. They felt that it prevented Harrison from interacting in a more meaningful way with peers. They also felt that he was "in his own world" on the computer. Harrison's parents were pretty confused about it all. They agreed with both perspectives, and saw the merits of both opinions. However, they felt that Harrison could not survive without the computer at home.

The team decided to use the computer to address some of Harrison's other goals in an attempt to see if this strength could be applied in a context that was not so self-directed. The speech therapist decided to use the computer for some of her communication goals, and the teacher began to integrate one other child into Harrison's computer time once a day. She would structure the task in a turn-taking format. At home, Harrison's parents decided to reduce his access to the computer to ensure that he had access to other activities as well. They worked with the staff members to teach Harrison how to follow a photographic activity schedule.

As Harrison tolerated less free access and more structured activities on the computer, it became possible to modify his access and use of it to a much greater extent.

Planning for an Effective Team

To be as effective as possible, teams should meet regularly. Further, it is helpful to have an agenda, to meet in a conducive environment, and to have a leader who guides the discussions and keeps the group on track. Effective teams have members who participate, who support one another, and who work through conflict in a proactive manner (Amason et al, 1995).

Stephen Covey (1989) outlines several characteristics that can help ensure teams work effectively and efficiently together. He describes the importance of seeking first to understand, and then to be understood. Good teams are comprised of effective listeners, who can hear what their colleagues are saying and respond with empathy, compassion, respect, and determination to jointly address the problem. Covey also discusses synergy, the concept that the whole is greater than the sum of its parts. When teams come together in a spirit of mutual respect, and explore divergent thoughts and perspectives, the result is often richer, better, and more complete than it would have been with fewer members or less exploration of options.

An effective team is made, not born. A number of characteristics will help the team to develop cohesiveness, increase respect for one another, and solve problems effectively.

1. **Shared Goals and Vision**

    A team must have a sense of mission and purpose. What are the goals for this learner? What are his or her strengths and challenges? What can the team do to maximize the student's success? Do we as members of the team share goals? Do we have the same view of this learner and of where we are going? Do we agree on how to help this learner on his journey?

ASID was a kindergarten student with severe social anxiety, who was very much an academic success. The team was in agreement that the first order was to reduce Asid's anxiety of being in the classroom. They did not initially concern themselves with whether he answered questions, greeted peers, or spoke at a comprehensible volume. They focused only on whether he was able to be present in the activities and on his levels of anxious behaviors (crying, picking his skin, and lip biting). When these behaviors were reduced to near zero levels, they slowly began to address other issues.

2. **Clear Role Definitions**

    An effective team is a well-defined team. Every member has his or her specific tasks and fulfills them. There is little ambiguity about who does what. That is, while role assignments should not be rigid, they must be clear.

EMMA'S family was a little unsure of how things would work once she was out of the specialized preschool she had attended for the past two years. They wondered who would convey information to them about Emma's day, who would assist them in preparing Emma for upcoming events and lessons, and how the shadow's and the teacher's roles would be differentiated. They were greatly relieved, therefore, when they were given a sample of a daily note that would be filled out every day jointly by the teacher and the shadow. They were also given times when they could call the teacher if they had any special concerns, a notebook to use for daily communication with the teacher and the shadow, and a schedule of team meetings where they would have access to all of the professionals involved with Emma.

3. Effective Communication

An effective team communicates openly, honestly, directly, and respectfully. Team members do not inhibit divergent opinions, but voice and support them in the spirit of team-work. Team members do not withdraw from discussions, but participate, even when opinions are discrepant.

SAM had difficulty socially on the playground, but the members of his team had very different opinions about why he was struggling. His teacher felt that Sam was overwhelmed by the noise and action on the playground, and suggested shortening the time to help build a tolerance for the action on the playground. His parents thought Sam was not comfortable with school yet, as he didn't even know all of the kids' names. His speech therapist thought that Sam might be having trouble using his language in the playground setting, especially if he was anxious.

Faced with this range of opinions, the team collected some more specific data on how Sam was struggling on the playground. A pattern emerged of difficulty interacting with unfamiliar children, especially when he was engaged in a preferred activity. Sam would scream or throw things when people invited him to do something else or asked for a turn on his preferred activity. The team decided to increase Sam's familiarity with peers (by teaching their names, initiating greetings with them, etc.) and to give him ways to express his desire to continue with preferred activities (e.g., saying, "In a minute … "). They actively practiced giving up the preferred activity, so that others could get turns, first with adults in analog situations (contrived situations that mirror reality, but in which variables can be more easily controlled), and later with peers.

4. Ongoing Dialogue

An effective team manages conflict by continuing to work through divergent opinions. Team members may collect data to guide a choice, ensuring that the decision is accurate and correct for an individual learner.

SUE-LING was very much into brushing, and liked to be brushed by her OT and other members of the team. Some members of the team felt brushing was meeting an important sensory need, whereas others thought Sue-Ling simply liked the attention, but didn't need the brushing per se with such a high frequency.

The team collected data (guided by a behavior specialist). They took data on Sue-Ling's self-stimulatory behavior and on her academic accuracy in work sessions preceded by either a brushing session or interaction with a teacher. They found that Sue-Ling's self-stimula-

tory behavior was less and her accuracy was higher after brushing, substantiating the hypothesis that brushing was serving some purpose. However, they found that her accuracy was even higher and her behaviors even lower following interaction. The team decided to increase her non-contingent access to attention in an attempt to increase her academic achievement and reduce her self-stimulatory behaviors.

Each member of an educational team has a unique perspective, unique experiences, and unique expertise. Effective teams recognize this, value each member's opinions and suggestions, and learn from one another. Creating opportunities to observe different team members in action can strengthen the skills of the entire team.

MEGAN, a first-year para, wasn't really sure how to help Ethan through a meltdown. She had read the behavior plan, and heard stories from the other members of the team. It was only when she observed the teacher actively working through a period of agitation with Ethan that it started to make sense. She saw how the teacher moved closer when Ethan began to get agitated. She watched her present Ethan with a visual explanation of the expectations (on a chart). Specifically, she saw how Ethan was told that if he could complete two more spelling words, he could go on the computer. She felt more confident about how to do those things once she saw them in action.

5. Reinforcement

Effective teams reinforce members for their efforts. When one member of a team does an extraordinary job, her effort is noticed and recognized. When the student makes progress, the team takes a moment to celebrate the success. The team focuses on savoring the progress and the triumphs, and on recognizing how the team has helped bring good outcomes to fruition.

VERA'S team starts every meeting with each team member sharing a "best moment" of the week. It helps to give all members of the team information on how Vera is doing in multiple contexts, and it gives everyone a regular opportunity to celebrate the good moments, progress, and successes.

6. **Effective Problem Solving**
   Effective teams manage problems with efficiency, determination, and logic. They utilize the steps of successful problem solving: identify problems, generate alternative solutions, anticipate the likely consequences for each course of action, and choose the best alternative.

ERIK'S team had to decide what to do about his difficulties in managing cafeteria noise. They considered several solutions. If they kept him in the lunchroom and worked through the difficulties, he would likely escalate in his behavioral episodes, and peers might become frightened or avoidant. If they removed him and arranged for him to eat lunch alone, they would also remove any opportunity for social engagement during a prime time for such activity.

After considering the various options, they decided to form a "lunch bunch," whereby several children accompanied Erik for lunch in another room. This arrangement gave the teacher a chance to focus on social skill development during lunch. It also increased Erik's familiar-

ity with several students. Students were eager to volunteer to be part of the "lunch bunch" as it was a novel and attention-rich experience for them, and the peers' parents were very open to this type of helping experience for their children.

7. Positivity

Effective teams view events as challenges, as opposed to catastrophes, meeting challenges with a "can do" attitude. They tend to be optimistic about their learner, about their learner's successes, and about resolving any problems that arise.

LINDSEY'S team was not daunted by her difficult first week at school. Recognizing the huge adjustment she was undergoing, they increased support within the classroom for the first month, tracked data closely, increased communication with the child's parents, and proceeded calmly into the second week. Soon Lindsey started to settle in.

8. Flexibility

Effective teams are flexible. They recognize that change is inevitable, that teams are dynamic, and that plans must be constantly varied and altered to adjust to circumstances. While role definition is important, members of effective teams readily assist one another in picking up responsibilities when circumstances warrant it.

CHRISTOPHER'S classroom teacher realized that she could not complete the daily note to Christopher's parents before the children left for the day without jeopardizing other aspects of the classroom schedule. She had considered writing the note before the after-noon's academic subjects, but that would not work, as data from that part of the day would then be missing from the form.

After considering the options, she asked Chris's shadow to complete the information and show it to her at the end of the day. In this way, the teacher could add any missing information, but in a much more time-efficient manner. The shadow was happy to assist in the process, and the parents received a much more detailed note.

WHAT MAKES FOR EFFECTIVE TEAMWORK? TOP LIST FOR EDUCATORS

- Shared goals and vision
- Clear role definitions
- Effective communication
- Ongoing dialogue

- Reinforcement
- Effective problem solving
- Positivity
- Flexibility

Planning for an Effective Team

Whenever there is a diversity of opinion and an effort to integrate perspectives, conflict may arise.

KENNY was having a very hard time since returning to school in September. He was not successfully integrating into group instruction time, and he seemed agitated on a regular basis. He was often biting his shirt, and he had chewed more than a dozen crayons and pencils into pieces. Other students were disturbed by his behavior, and his teachers were concerned from a sanitation and health per-

spective. Kenny's parents thought that the behavior was the result of sensory needs, and wanted Kenny to be given some other ways to get sensory needs met. The behavior analyst was concerned that Kenny was failing a lot in class, experiencing stigmatization, and receiving little reinforcement. Her recommendation was to decrease inclusion time, plan inclusion around preferred activities, and try to get some control over the target behaviors in 1:1 instruction. The teacher felt strongly that reducing Kenny's time in class was a bad idea; she felt he would know he got away with getting out of hard activities through negative behaviors.

At their team meetings, discussions were heated, and issues remained unresolved. No one felt heard by the other members of the team, and everyone was frustrated. Another professional joined the team to assist them in resolving their conflicts and to develop goals for Kenny. This professional helped the team members to articulate their views, listen responsively to one another, and work together to compromise and collaborate.

Conflict, in and of itself, is not undesirable in the context of a team. Conflict can be productive as it builds cohesiveness, increases the involvement of its members, and results in positive resolutions (Capozzoli, 1995). Conflict can be an opportunity for personal growth and learning for each individual member as well (Banner, 1996). Problem-solving techniques may be used to help the team to navigate the disagreement by exploring the various options and their likely effects and choosing the best option.

Kenny's team used problem solving effectively. Each recommendation was examined in terms of its likely outcomes. For example, leaving Kenny in the room full-time (as the teacher preferred) would likely result in more agitation, more peer avoidance, and more broken crayons. Taking him out of the room for much of the day would likely result in more learning, less agitation, more opportunities to work on difficult behaviors in controlled settings, and more successful inclusion experiences.

However, conflict can also become counterproductive. When that happens, conflict is characterized by hostility, distrust, apathy, and the obstruction of open communication.

KENNY'S team was (thankfully) able to avert this course of action. However, the team was on the way to very negative outcomes. Team members had begun criticizing each other outside the classroom. Some team members were beginning to skip meetings, because nothing ever got resolved anyway.

What is important about conflict is how it is managed (Amason et al., 1995). The type of conflict that can be helpful is conflict that explores different alternatives, innovative solutions, and creative problem solving. Frank discussions about such options build understanding and commitment to the team's goals and decision (Amason et al., 1995).

Summary

In the absence of effective teamwork, even the best laid plans may only be minimally effective. Teamwork is the cornerstone to making it all work. An essential aspect of teamwork, especially when working with young children, is parent-professional collaboration. Parents and professionals must respect each other's expertise, opinions, and input. Communication, a focus on the positive, and respect for divergent perspectives all enhance the parent-professional partnership. In the larger team context, every member of the team has unique expertise and opinions that can enhance the success of educational efforts. Conflict is inevitable even on an otherwise successful team. The key is to view it as a chance for growth and increased cohesiveness. Sharing a vision and clearly delineating roles and responsibilities will enhance the effectiveness of teams. Positivity, flexibility, and creative problem solving help teams manage more challenging dilemmas and discussions.

Chapter 6

CASE STUDIES

The following case scenarios illustrate some of the wide differences that exist among children with ASD. The two children featured here have significant strengths and tremendous challenges. The first scenario, Henry, tells the story of a unique and intelligent little boy whose idiosyncrasies and rigidities intensified during his toddler and preschool years. His diagnosis of HFA helped to identify some of his needs.

The second scenario, Jésus, tells the story of an intense but very bright boy with AS, whose screaming, social isolation, and unusual interests made it very difficult for him to succeed in school. The central message is not about their diagnoses per se (e.g., HFA vs. AS), as they shared many characteristics, and were helped through similar interventions. A variety of strategies outlined throughout this book helped both of these boys to be more comfortable and more successful.

Henry

Henry was an unusual toddler, but no one in his family was especially concerned about him. His language developed slowly, with little language his first 18 months. After that, his language continued to develop, although he did not always use it in typical ways. In particular, he had atypical ways to describe significant others. He referred to his younger sister as "poopie," which probably had originated as a reference to a need for a diaper change. He referred to his grandmother as "Maryland," referring to the state where she lived. Everyone thought Henry's idiosyncrasies were charming.

Henry showed an amazing ability to memorize. He knew all the words to every Beach Boys song (his parents' favorite group), and often charmed friends and family by dancing while singing along.

His parents were especially amazed at his ability to read without training. At age 2, he began to refer to common grocery items by their brand names. He called orange juice "Minute Maid," graham crackers "Nabisco," and macaroni and cheese "Kraft." He also started reading street signs, commenting in car rides, "Washington Avenue," and so on.

When he was 2-1/2, the family started wondering about Henry. They saw that he was very isolated at family and neighborhood gatherings. They began to have trouble interrupting his singing concerts and meeting his demands to listen to Beach Boys tunes all the time. They also noticed he scripted lines from movies and songs. While the comments were sometimes relevant to the context, often they were not. Finally, Henry, who had always been a picky eater, started eating less and less. He was mostly drinking, and only from a bottle. He would eat bananas, but only in the grocery store. He would eat yogurt, but only on the steps going to his room.

His parents brought their son to his pediatrician, who reassured them that it probably wasn't anything serious, but did refer them to a pediatric neurologist. While waiting for this appointment, they also made an appointment with a specialist in autism spectrum disorders. At this appointment, the psychologist suggested that Henry might meet the criteria for an autism spectrum disorder. The psychologist offered that Henry might be a high-functioning child with autism, and that his idiosyncrasies and rigidities, even his excellent reading abilities, might be indicative of autism.

Just before he turned 3, Henry began an intensive home-based ABA program for 40 hours per week. His parents wanted to be as aggressive as possible in intervening, and they felt he had an excellent chance of making good progress with a high level of treatment. Sure enough, Henry made rapid gains. He was able to learn very readily, and did not require repetition to learn. He also generalized skills without special training. These were tremendous strengths, and the behavior analyst overseeing the case emphasized this to his parents.

Nevertheless, there were struggles. Henry's eating habits declined further. His family attempted to make access to milk contingent on eating solid food. This strategy failed, and put dehydration on the list of his parents' fears. They also created a program to desensitize Henry to the sights, smells, and textures of foods. At first, Henry was rewarded just for having food present, then for touching it. It was a slow and painful process, with medical concerns growing as he failed to gain weight and grow in stature. High-calorie supplements were added to his milk.

At the same time, Henry became more rigid. He created lots of rules about everything. Staff members and his parents had to be constantly on the lookout for new routines, which would then become ingrained. He wanted to enter the car only on the left side. He wanted to put all the Little People in particular seats on the toy bus. He wanted to tell stories on the felt board with no variation in theme, or even in wording. In fact, his excellent memory became an impediment to learning, as he tried to recreate every action, trip, or story verbatim and exactly as presented.

A variety of strategies were put in place to help Henry adapt to variability and to demonstrate flexibility. He was rewarded at all times for tolerating change of any type. He would have access to Beach Boys songs contingent on demonstrating such flexibility. Staff members also created Social Stories™ about nearly everything. (They had to create at least three versions of each story to address memorization and ritual retelling.) He was also permitted to be rigid about a few things. For example, he was allowed to arrange and rearrange Disney characters on his dresser, and he was allowed to read certain books every night.

Slowly, he became more flexible. After a year of home-based intervention, the team agreed that it was time to address Henry's social deficits. He went to a preschool with a shadow. His family chose to simply describe Henry to the staff there as "a late bloomer," who had begun speaking late. While Henry generally did fine in this setting, he was socially isolated. The shadow worked to create social opportunities. However, Henry was not always reinforcing to interact with. He could be very intrusive with peers, especially when he did not agree with how they were playing. He also became totally fixated on the reward system they were using at the preschool. He wanted to see the card on which the shadow recorded his token earnings, and he debated about whether tokens had been earned. Eventually, the system itself became a source of disruption, and the team had to alter it in a number of ways. First, they had to build up his tolerance for delay in feedback. They also had to work on increasing the subtlety of the feedback he was given.

His rigidity with peers was a significant problem. He required practice sessions at home to increase flexibility. In particular, his rules about how to play with toys were a stubborn problem. Staff members in the home program worked on building his tolerance for the ideas of others, and taught him to comment on or narrate the play of others. This gave him a way to interact with peers that was nondirective.

Shadows also worked on building his self-management skills. For example, they began having Henry rate himself on target areas at the end of the day. He received bonus rewards when his reports were especially accurate. A sample of his daily sheet is listed on the following page.

Daily Sheet for Henry

2 pts: no reminders
1 pt: with 1 reminder
0 points: more than 1 reminder
Bonus: 2 points if agree

JOB	SHADOW	PTS	HENRY	BONUS	TOTAL
Listen to teacher					
Follow the rules					
Let friends choose					
Talk with friends					
Finish snack					

Henry's shadow was faded over almost two years and, as a result, he went to kindergarten without a shadow. In kindergarten he had little difficulty, and was viewed as very smart by his teachers. He began to show real giftedness in music and math during the first years of school.

Henry recalls some of his experiences during his earlier years. He remembers being obsessed with and excited by reading street signs. He remembers that a lot of people taught him to speak and play.

Jésus

Jésus was unusual from the start. He was a difficult, colicky baby. He did not just have colicky periods; it seemed he was almost always unhappy. It was difficult to soothe him, and often he cried despite all efforts to calm him. He did not nurse well and was switched to formula, which also did not help. In a word: His infancy was difficult.

No wonder Jésus became an intense toddler. He had very extreme tantrums, usually when things did not go his way. Sometimes his parents could not figure out why he was upset, but most of the time they could identify a trigger. The main problem was that they couldn't calm him easily, even when they understood why he was upset.

Jésus was very bright. That was very clear. His language was extraordinary, and he grasped concepts well beyond his months and years. He knew all his letters and numbers by age 1, and he was reading at age 2. His parents began to see that he might be gifted. He was not interested in the things other kids enjoyed. While other young children were interested in Thomas the Tank Engine, he preferred studying the engineering details of steam locomotives. He also studied maps of old railroad routes and various types and makes of steam locomotives. While other kids his age enjoyed playing in the sprinkler, he preferred discussing how the water moved through pipes into people's homes and sprinklers.

He really enjoyed speaking with others about steam locomotives and about pipes. His parents thought it was unusual, but also kind of adorable. They knew that it was related to his high intelligence, and they understood that his brilliance made it hard for him to relate to age peers. They eagerly awaited his entrance into school, hoping it would provide a much-needed intellectual outlet for their son. At home, they continued to struggle with Jésus's intensity. He screamed at the top of his lungs for long periods when he became agitated, just as he had when he was a toddler.

Jésus did exceptionally well in school in many ways, and his teacher was impressed with his cognitive skills. During his whole first year, he excelled in every area of the curriculum. Initially, and increasingly during the year, though, the teacher mentioned that Jésus had some social difficulties. She described Jésus as immature in his play and as unaware of other kids' feelings. For example, she commented on how he frequently walked into the block structures created by other students without noticing their projects and without remorse. She said he could be aggressive with his peers, especially if they encroached on his area, or tried to play alongside him. She also noted that Jésus frequently spoke about wanting to be a computer or a pipe, expressing concern over such unusual (and asocial) goals. Finally, she mentioned the screaming. Some of the screaming happened in predictable places or contexts, such as in the cafeteria or during a fire drill (presumably because of the noise). At other times, the reactions were prompted by very minor events or unknown events. The teacher was concerned about the intensity of his angry reactions, and reported that he was very difficult to calm at those times. After Jésus's parents spoke to the teacher, they mentioned her concerns to their pediatrician.

A developmental pediatrician diagnosed Jésus as having Asperger Syndrome. When the doctor explained the symptoms to Jésus's parents, the pieces of the puzzle started to fall into place for them. However, it was difficult to imagine how they should try to help him. Unlike many other children on the autism spectrum, Jésus did not need a special school, a shadow, or a special education classroom. What did he need?

His parents spent the remainder of the school year looking for alternatives for Jésus. They found a small preschool with many gifted children that were willing to accept him. They felt he might do better in a smaller environment, with a lower student-to-staff ratio. Jésus did do much better. A major bonus of the setting was the presence of other gifted students. The boredom that had been a factor in the previous preschool was no longer an issue, as Jésus found similarly minded individuals. One of the boys was also very interested in trains. He was especially interested in Amtrak schedules and which type of Amtrak trains went on which tracks at what times. While this was different than Jésus's area of interest, it was similar enough to create a bond. Soon they became train friends.

By the time Jésus was ready to enter kindergarten, further interests evolved for which a community existed. Jésus became very interested in chess, and found a boy in the class to play it with. He also developed an interest in the solar system, and found a classmate who was very interested in the Hubbell telescope.

Jésus required a lot of supports to be successful in preschool and kindergarten, including clear rules, behavior contracts, and incentive systems. He responded well to relaxation training, and learned some exercises that could be used in his states of agitation. He was also responsive to sensory intervention. Regular access to deep pressure and to gross-motor activity reduced his episodes of agitation markedly. And he was very responsive to self-management, including tracking his own behavior and reporting on the extent to which he fulfilled his behavioral contracts.

In addition to these supports, certain accommodations greatly reduced Jésus's level of anxiety and his behavioral disruptiveness. He was permitted to skip lunch in the cafeteria and assemblies in the auditorium, and his attention and behavior were much better when he took hourly breaks in the gym.

As Jésus gets a bit older there are worries that he will be the victim of bullying, and his teachers are trying to brainstorm about how to help address that. They are planning to teach him assertiveness skills, decision making about when to tell a teacher, and skills in discerning when to listen to peers. It is also increasingly important to Jésus that he knows kids like himself, and his parents and teachers are working to create and maintain connections with peers he can relate to.

Factors That Were Important for Jésus's Success

- Recognizing social isolation preference
- Finding strengths
- Accommodations
- Sensory outlets
- Self-management

Summary

As illustrated in the case studies in this chapter, the unique needs of young children with autism spectrum disorders can be met in early childhood settings, given the following conditions:

- caring and knowledgeable staff

- an effective educational team

- close and ongoing parent-staff communication

- proper assessment

- careful program planning

- ongoing data collection followed by program changes/ adjustments, when appropriate

- use of best-practice interventions

- a supportive environment that takes into consideration the child's sensory, cognitive, motor and other needs

The previous chapters in this book have addressed each of these issues, thus helping to ensure the best possible outcomes for our young learners.

REFERENCES

Alavosius, M. P., & Sulzer-Azaroff, B. (1986). The effects of performance feedback on the safety of client lifting and transfer. *Journal of Applied Behavior Analysis, 19,* 261-267.

Amason, A. C., Thompson, K. T., Hochwarter, W. A., & Harrison, A. W. (1995). Conflict: An important dimension in successful management teams. *Organizational Dynamics, 24,* 20-35.

Aspy, R., & Grossman, B. (2007a). *Underlying Characteristics Checklist: A needs assessment tool to facilitate intervention design for individuals with autism spectrum disorders.* Shawnee Mission, KS: Autism Asperger Publishing Company.

Aspy, R., & Grossman, B. G. (2007b). *The Ziggurat model: A framework for designing comprehensive interventions for individuals with high-functioning autism and Asperger Syndrome.* Shawnee Mission, KS: Autism Asperger Publishing Company.

Ayers, A. J. (1979). *Sensory integration and the child.* Los Angeles: Western Psychological Services.

Baker, J. E. (2002). *Social skills training for children and adolescents with Asperger Syndrome and social-communication problems.* Shawnee Mission, KS: Autism Asperger Publishing Company.

Baker, J. E. (2003). *The social skills picture book: Teaching, play, emotion, and communication to children with autism.* Arlington, TX: Future Horizons.

Baker, M. (2000). Incorporating the thematic ritualistic behaviors of children with autism into games: Increasing social play interactions with siblings. *Journal of Positive Behavior Interventions, 2,* 66-84.

Banner, D. K. (1996). Conflict resolution: A recontextualization. *Leadership and Organization Development Journal, 16,* 31-34.

Baron-Cohen, S. (1997). *Mindblindness: An essay on autism and theory of mind.* Cambridge, MA: MIT Press.

Baron-Cohen, S., Allen, J., & Gillberg, C. (1992). Can autism be detected at 18 months? The needle, the haystack, and the CHAT. *British Journal of Psychiatry, 161,* 839-843.

Baron-Cohen, S., Cox, A., Baird, G., Swettenham, J., Nightingale, N., Morgan, K., Drew, A., & Charman, T. (1996). Psychological markers in the detection of autism in infancy in a large population. *British Journal of Psychiatry, 168,* 158-163.

Binder, C. (1996). Behavioral fluency: Evolution of a new paradigm. *The Behavior Analyst, 19,* 163-197.

Buron, K. D. (2006). *When my worries get too big! A relaxation book for children who live with anxiety.* Shawnee Mission, KS: Autism Asperger Publishing Company.

Buron, K. D., & Curtis, M. (2003). *The incredible 5-point scale: Assisting students with autism spectrum disorders in understanding social interactions and controlling their emotional responses.* Shawnee Mission, KS: Autism Asperger Publishing Company.

Butterworth, G. (1991). *The ontogeny and phylogeny of joint visual attention.* In A. Whiten (Ed.), *Natural theories of mind* (pp. 223-232). Oxford, UK: Blackwell.

Capozzoli, T. K. (1995). Conflict resolution: A key ingredient in successful teams. *Supervision, 15,* 3-6.

Cardon, T. (2004). *Let's talk emotions: Helping children with social cognitive deficits, including AS, HFA, and NVLD, learn to understand and express empathy and emotions.* Shawnee Mission, KS: Autism Asperger Publishing Company.

Cardon, T. (2007). *Initiations and interactions: Early intervention techniques for parents of children with autism spectrum disorders.* Shawnee Mission, KS: Autism Asperger Publishing Company.

Carr, E. G., & Darcy, M. (1990). Setting generality of peer modeling in children with autism. *Journal of Autism and Developmental Disorders, 20,* 45-59.

Carr, E. G., & Durand, V. M. (1985). Reducing behavior problems through functional communication training. *Journal of Applied Behavior Analysis, 18*(2), 111-126.

Carter, M., & Santomauro, J. (2004). *Space travelers: An interactive program for developing social understanding, social competence, and social skills for students with Asperger Syndrome, autism, and other social challenges.* Shawnee Mission, KS: Autism Asperger Publishing Company.

Carter, M., & Santomauro, J. (2007). *Pirates: An early years group program for developing social understanding and social competence for children with autism and related challenges.* Shawnee Mission, KS: Autism Asperger Publishing Company.

Cavallaro, C. C., & Haney, M. (1999). *Preschool inclusion.* Baltimore: Paul H. Brookes Publishing Co.

Celiberti, D. A., & Harris, S. L. (1993). The effects of a play skills intervention for siblings of children with autism. *Behavior Therapy, 24,* 573-599.

Cooper, J. O., Heron, T. E., & Heward, W. L. (1987). *Applied behavior analysis.* Upper Saddle River, NJ: Prentice-Hall.

Cooper, J. O., Heron, T. E., & Heward, W. L. (2007). *Applied behavior analysis* (2nd ed.). Upper Saddle River, NJ: Prentice-Hall.

Covey, S. R. (1989). *The seven habits of highly effective people.* New York: Simon & Schuster.

Demchak, M., & Drinkwater, S. (1992). Preschoolers with severe disabilities: The case against segregation. *Topics in Early Childhood Special Education, 11,* 70-83.

Dewey, M. (1991). Autism and Asperger's Syndrome. In U. Frith (Ed.), *Autism and Asperger syndrome* (pp. 184-206). London: Cambridge University Press.

Dougherty, K. M., & Johnston, J. M. (1996). Overlearning, fluency, and automaticity. *The Behavior Analyst, 19,* 289-292.

Doyle, M. B. (1997). *The paraprofessionals guide to the inclusive classroom.* Baltimore: Paul H. Brookes Publishing Co.

Ducharme, J. M., & Feldman, M. A. (1992). Comparison of staff training strategies to promote generalized teaching skills. *Journal of Applied Behavior Analysis, 25,* 165-179.

Duker, P. C., Sigafoos, J., Barron, J., & Coleman, F. (1998). The Motivation Assessment Scale: Reliability and construct validity across three topographies of behavior. *Research in Developmental Disabilities, 19*(2), 131-141.

Dunlap, G. (1984). The influence of task variation and maintenance tasks on the learning of autistic children. *Journal of Experimental Child Psychology, 37,* 41-64.

Dunlap, G., Hieneman, M., Knoster, T., Fox, L., Anderson, J., & Albin, R. W. (2000). Essential elements of inservice training in positive behavior support. *Journal of Positive Behavior Interventions, 2,* 22-32.

Dunn, W. (1999a). *The Sensory Profile: A contextual measure of children's responses to sensory experiences in daily life.* San Antonio, TX: The Psychological Corporation.

Dunn, W. (1999b). *Short Sensory Profile.* San Antonio, TX: The Psychological Corporation.

Durand, V. M., & Crimmins, D. B. (1987). Assessment and treatment of psychotic speech in an autistic child. *Journal of Autism and Developmental Disabilities, 17*(1), 17-28.

Durand, V. M., & Crimmins, D. B. (1988). Identifying the variables maintaining self-injurious behavior. *Journal of Autism and Developmental Disorders, 18,* 99-117.

Elliot, C. (1990). *Differential Ability Scales.* San Antonio, TX: Psychological Corporation.

Espin, R. (2003). *Amazingly ... Alphie.* Shawnee Mission, KS: Autism Asperger Publishing Company.

Etzel, B. C., & LeBlanc, J. M. (1979). The simplest treatment alternative: The law of parsimony applied to choosing appropriate instructional control and errorless learning procedures for the difficult-to-teach child. *Journal of Autism and Developmental Disorders, 9,* 361-382.

Fabrizio, M. A., & Moors, A. L. (2003). Evaluating mastery: Measuring instructional outcomes for children with autism. *European Journal of Behavior Analysis, 4,* 23-36.

Fenske, E. C., Krantz, P. J., & McClannahan, L. E. (2001). Incidental teaching: A not-so-discrete-trial teaching procedure. In C. Maurice, G. Green, & R. M. Foxx (Eds.), *Making a difference: Behavioral intervention for autism* (pp. 75-82). Austin, TX: Pro-Ed.

Fisher, W. W., Piazza, C. C., Bowman, L. G., & Amari, A. (1996). Integrating caregiver report with a systematic choice assessment to enhance reinforcer identification. *American Journal of Mental Retardation, 101,* 15-25.

Gagnon, E. (2001). *Power Cards: Using special interests to motivate children and youth with Asperger Syndrome and autism.* Shawnee Mission, KS: Autism Asperger Publishing Company.

Gilliam, J. E. (1995). *Gilliam Autism Rating Scale.* Austin, TX: Pro-Ed.

Gilliam, J. E., & McConnell, K. S. (1997). *Scales for Predicting Successful Inclusion*. Austin, Texas: Pro-Ed.

Gray, C. (1993). *The original Social Story™ book*. Arlington, TX: Future Horizons.

Gray, C. (1994). *The new social story book*. Arlington, TX: Future Horizons.

Green, S. K., & Shinn, M. R. (1994). Parent attitudes about special education and reintegration: What is the role of student outcomes? *Exceptional Children, 61,* 269-281.

Guralnick, M. J., Connor, R. T., & Hammond, M. (1995). Parent perspectives of peer relationships and friendships in integrated and specialized programs. *American Journal of Mental Retardation, 99,* 457-476.

Gutstein, S. E. (2000). *Autism/Aspergers: Solving the relationship puzzle*. Arlington, TX: Future Horizons.

Gutstein, S. E., & Sheely, R. K. (2002). *Relationship development intervention with young children: Social and emotional development activities for Asperger Syndrome, autism, PDD, and NLD*. Philadelphia: Jessica Kingsley Publishers.

Happé, F.G.E. (1994). An advanced test of theory of mind: Understanding of story characters' thoughts by able autistic, mentally handicapped, and normal children and adults. *Journal of Autism and Developmental Disorders, 24,* 129-154.

Happé, F.G.E., Ehlers, S., Fletcher, S., Frith, U., Johannsson, M., Gillberg, C. et al. (1996). Theory of mind in the brain: Evidence from a PET scan study of Asperger syndrome. *Neuroreport, 8,* 197-201.

Harris, S. L., & Handleman, J. S. (1997). Helping children with autism enter the mainstream. In D. J. Cohen & F. R. Volkmar (Eds.), *Handbook of autism and pervasive developmental disorders* (2nd ed., pp. 665-675). New York: John Wiley & Sons, Inc.

Harris, S. L., Handleman, J. S., Belchic, J., & Glasberg, B. (1995). The Vineland Adaptive Behavior Scales for young children with autism. *Special Services in the Schools, 10*(1), 45-54.

Harris, S. L., & Weiss, M. J. (2007). *Right from the start: Behavioral intervention for young children with autism.* Bethesda, MD: Woodbine House.

Hart, B. M., & Risley, T. R. (1982). *How to use incidental teaching for elaborating language.* Austin, TX: Pro-Ed.

Hill, E. L., & Frith, U. (2003). Understanding autism: Insights from mind and brain. In U. Frith & E. L. Hill (Eds.), *Autism: Mind and brain* (pp. 1-20). New York: Oxford University Press.

Iwata, B. A. (2002). *The Functional Analysis Screening Tool.* Gainesville; University of Florida Center on Self-Injury.

Iwata, B. A., & DeLeon, I. G. (1995). *The Functional Analysis Screening Tool* (FAST). Unpublished manuscript, University of Florida, Gainesville.

Iwata, B. A., Dorsey, M. F., Slifer, K. J., Bauman, K. E., & Richman, G. S. (1994). Toward a functional analysis of self-injury. *Journal of Applied Behavior Analysis, 27*(2), 197-209.

Kasari, C., Sigman, M., Mundy, P., & Yirmiya, N. (1990). Affective sharing in the context of joint attention interactions of normal, autistic, and mentally retarded children. *Journal of Autism and Developmental Disorders, 20,* 87-100.

Kaufman, A. S., & Kaufman, N. L. (1983). *The Kaufman Assessment Battery for Children.* Circle Pines, MN: American Guidance Services.

Keating-Velasco, J. (2007). *A is for autism, F is for friend.* Shawnee Mission, KS: Autism Asperger Publishing Company.

Kincaid, D., Knoster, T., Harrower, J. K., Shannon, P., & Bustamante, S. (2002). Measuring the impact of positive behavior support. *Journal of Positive Behavior Interventions, 4,* 109-117.

Koegel, R. L., & Koegel, L. K. (1995). *Teaching children with autism: Strategies for initiating positive interactions and improving learning opportunities.* Baltimore: Paul H. Brookes Publishing Co.

Koegel, R. L. & Koegel, L. K. (2005). *Pivotal response treatments for autism: Communication, social, and academic development.* Baltimore: Paul H. Brookes Publishing Co.

Koegel, R. L., Koegel, L. K., & Surrat, A. (1992). Language intervention and disruptive behavior in preschool children with autism. *Journal of Autism and Developmental Disorders, 22,* 141-153.

Koegel, R. L., O'Dell, M. C., & Koegel, L. K. (1987). A natural language teaching paradigm for nonverbal autistic children. *Journal of Autism and Developmental Disorders, 17,* 187-200.

Koegel, R. L., Russo, D. C., & Rincover, A. (1977). Assessing and training teachers in the generalized use of behavior modification with autistic children. *Journal of Applied Behavior Analysis, 10,* 197-205.

Krug, D. A., Arick, J., & Almond, P. (1980). Behavior checklist for identifying severely handicapped individuals with high levels of autistic behavior. *Journal of Child Psychology and Psychiatry, 21,* 221-229.

Kutter, S., Myles, B. S., & Carlson, J. K. (1998). The use of Social Stories™ to reduce precursors to tantrum behavior in a student with autism. *Focus on Autism and Other Developmental Disabilities, 13,* 176-182.

Lancioni, G. E., & Smeets, P. M. (1986). Procedures and parameters of errorless discrimination training with developmentally impaired individuals. In N. R. Ellis & N. W. Bray (Eds.), *International review of research in mental retardation* (Volume 14, pp. 135-164). Orlando, FL: Academic Press.

Laski, K. E., Charlop, M. H., & Schreibman, L. (1988). Training parents to use the natural language paradigm to increase their children's speech. *Journal of Applied Behavior Analysis, 21,* 391-400.

LeCouteur, A., Lord, C., & Rutter, M. (2002). *The Autism Diagnostic Interview – Revised.* Los Angeles: Western Psychological Services.

Levy, A., & Dawson, G. (1992). Social stimulation and joint attention in young autistic children. *Journal of Abnormal Child Psychology, 20, 555-566.*

Lifter, K. (2000). Linking assessment to intervention for children with developmental disabilities and at-risk for developmental delay: The Developmental Play Assessment Instrument. In K. Gitlin-Weiner, A. Sandgrund, & C. Schafer (Eds.), *Play diagnosis and assessment* (2nd ed., pp. 228-261). New York: John Wiley & Sons.

Lifter, K., Sulzer-Azaroff, B., Anderson, S., & Cowdery, G. (1993). Teaching play activities to preschool children with disabilities: The impact of developmental considerations. *Journal of Early Intervention, 17,* 139-159.

Lord, C., Rutter, M., DiLavore, P. D., & Risi, S. (2001). *Autism Diagnostic Observation Schedule.* Los Angeles: Western Psychological Services.

Lord, C., Rutter, M., & LeCouteur, A. (1994). Autism Diagnostic Interview: A revised version of a Diagnostic Interview for Caregivers of Individuals with Possible Pervasive Developmental Disorders. *Journal of Autism and Developmental Disorders, 24*(5), 659-685.

MacDuff, G. S., Krantz, P. J., & McClannahan, L. E. (2001). Prompts and prompt-fading strategies for people with autism. In C. Maurice, G. Green, & R. M. Foxx (Eds.), *Making a difference: Behavioral intervention for autism* (pp. 37-50). Austin, TX: Pro-Ed.

Manasco, K. (2006). *Way to A: Empowering children with autism spectrum and other neurological disorders to monitor and replace aggression and tantrum behavior.* Shawnee Mission, KS: Autism Asperger Publishing Company.

Maurice, C., Green, G., & Luce, S. (1996). *Behavioral intervention for young children with autism: A manual for parents and professionals.* Austin, TX: Pro-Ed.

McClannahan, L. E., & Krantz, P. J. (1993). On systems analysis in autism intervention programs. *Journal of Applied Behavior Analysis, 26,* 589-596.

McCracken, H. (2006). *That's what is different about me! Helping children understand autism spectrum disorders.* Shawnee Mission, KS: Autism Asperger Publishing Company.

McGee, G. G., Almeida, M. C., Sulzer-Azaroff, B., & Feldman, R. S. (1992). Prompting reciprocal interactions via peer incidental teaching. *Journal of Applied Behavior Analysis, 25,* 117-126.

Meiners, C. (2006). *Accept and value each person.* Minneapolis, MN: Free Spirit Publishing.

Meiners, C. (2006). *Reach out and give.* Minneapolis, MN: Free Spirit Publishing.

Merrell, K. W. (1994). *Kindergarten and preschool behavior scales.* Brandon, VT: Clinical Psychology Publishing Company.

Miltenberger, R. G. (1998). Methods for assessing antecedent influences on challenging behaviors. In J. K. Luiselli & M. J. Cameron (Eds.), *Antecedent control* (pp. 47-66). Baltimore: Paul H. Brookes Publishing Co.

Moore, S. T. (2002). *Asperger Syndrome and the elementary school experience: Practical solutions for academic and social difficulties.* Shawnee Mission, KS: Autism Asperger Publishing Company.

Mundy, P., Sigman, M., & Kasari, C. (1990). Longitudinal study of joint attention and language development in autistic children. *Journal of Autism and Developmental Disorders, 20,* 115-128.

Murrell, D. (2004). *Oliver Onion – The onion who learns to accept and be himself.* Shawnee Mission, KS: Autism Asperger Publishing Company.

Myles, B. S., Cook, K. T., Miller, N. E., Rinner, L., & Robbins, L. A. (2000). *Asperger Syndrome and sensory issues: Practical solutions for making sense of the world.* Shawnee Mission, KS: Autism Asperger Publishing Company.

Myles, B .S., & Southwick, J. (2005). *Asperger Syndrome and dif-ficult moments: Practical solutions for tantrums, rage, and melt-downs. Revised edition.* Shawnee Mission, KS: Autism Asperg-er Publishing Company.

Noell, G. H., Witt, J. C., LaFleur, L. H., Mortenson, B. P., Ranier, D. D., & LeVelle, J. (2000). Increasing intervention implementation in general education following consultation: A comparison of two follow-up strategies. *Journal of Applied Behavior Analysis, 33,* 271-284.

Odom, S. L., & Strain, P. S. (1986). A comparison of peer-initiation and teacher-antecedent intervention for promoting recipro-cal social interactions of autistic preschoolers. *Journal of Ap-plied Behavior Analysis, 19,* 59-71.

O'Neill, R. E., Horner, R. H., Albin, R. W., Sprague, J. R., Storey, K., & Newton, J. S. (1997). *Functional assessment and program development for problem behavior* (2nd ed.). Pacific Grove, CA: Brooks/Cole Publishing Company.

Ozonoff, S., Dawson, G., & McPartland, J. (2002). *A parent's guide to Asperger Syndrome and high-functioning autism.* New York: Guilford Press.

Parr, T. (2000). *The feelings book.* Boston: Little, Brown, and Company.

Parr, T. (2001). *It's ok to be different.* Boston: Little, Brown, and Com-pany.

Parr, T. (2002). *The feel good book.* Boston: Little, Brown, and Company.

Partington, J. W. (2006). *The Assessment of Basic Language and Learning Skills – Revised.* Pleasant Hill, CA: Behavior Analysts, Inc.

Partington, J. W., & Sundberg, M. L. (1998). *The Assessment of Basic Language and Learning Skills (The ABLLS).* Pleasant Hill, CA: Behavior Analysts Inc.

Peralta, S. (2002). *All about my brother.* Shawnee Mission, KS: Autism Asperger Publishing Company.

Pierce, K., & Schreibman, L. (1995). Increasing complex social behaviors in children with autism: Effects of peer-implemented pivotal response training. *Journal of Applied Behavior Analysis, 28,* 285-295.

Powers, M. (1997). Behavioral assessment of individuals with autism. In D. Cohen & F. Volkmar (Eds.), *Handbook of autism and pervasive developmental disorders* (pp. 448-459). New York: John Wiley & Sons.

Quill, K. A. (1995). *Teaching children with autism: Strategies to enhance communication and socialization.* New York: Delmar.

Quill, K. A. (2000). *Do-watch-listen-say: Social and communication intervention for children with autism.* Baltimore: Paul H. Brookes Publishing Co.

Quill, K. A., Bracken, K. N., & Fair, M. E. (2000). Assessment of social and communication skills for children with autism. In K. A. Quill, *Do-watch-listen-say: Social and communication intervention for children with autism.* Baltimore: Paul H. Brookes Publishing Co.

Reichart, D. C., Lynch, E. C., Anderson, B. C., Svobodny, L. A., DiCola, J. M., & Mercury, M. G. (1989). Parental perspectives on integrated preschool opportunities for children with handicaps and children without handicaps. *Journal of Early Intervention, 13,* 6-13.

Roid, G. (2003). *The Stanford-Binet Intelligence Scales – Fifth Edition*. Chicago: Riverside Publishing.

Rosenkoetter, S. E., Hains, A. H., & Fowler, S. A. (1994). *Bridging early services for children with special needs and their families: A practical guide for transition planning*. Baltimore: Paul H. Brookes Publishing Co.

Sansoti, F., Powell-Smith, K., & Kincaid, D. (2004). A research synthesis of social stories interventions for children with autism spectrum disorders. *Focus on Autism and Developmental Disabilities, 19*, 194-204.

Schepis, M. M., Reid, D. H., Ownbey, J., & Parsons, M. B. (2001). Training support staff to embed teaching within natural routines of young children with disabilities in an inclusive preschool. *Journal of Applied Behavior Analysis, 34*, 313-327.

Schertz, H. H., & Odom, S. L. (2004). Joint attention and early intervention with autism: A conceptual framework and promising approaches. *Journal of Early Intervention, 27*, 42-54.

Selinske, J. E., Greer, R. D., & Lodhi, S. (1991). A functional analysis of comprehensive application of behavior analysis to schooling. *Journal of Applied Behavior Analysis, 24*, 107-117.

Shure, M. B. (1992). *I can problem solve*. Champaign, IL: Research Press.

Sigman, M., & Kasari, C. (1995). Joint attention across contexts in normal and autistic children. In C. Moore & P. Dunham (Eds.), *Joint attention: Its origin and role in development* (pp. 189-204). Hillsdale, NJ: Earlbaum.

Simpson, R. L. (2005). *Autism spectrum disorders: Interventions and treatments for children and youth.* Thousand Oaks, CA: Corwin Press.

Skinner, B. F. (1957). *Verbal behavior.* New York: Appleton-Century-Crofts.

Snell, M. E., & Brown, F. (2000). *Instruction of students with severe handicaps.* Upper Saddle River, NJ: Prentice Hall.

Snell, M. E., & Janney, R. (2000). *Social relationships and peer support.* Baltimore: Paul H. Brookes Publishing Co.

Sparrow, S. S., Balla, D. A., & Cicchetti, D. V. (1984). *Vineland Adaptive Behavior Scales.* Circle Pines, MN: American Guidance Service.

Sparrow, S. S., Cicchetti, D. V. , & Balla, D. A. (2005). *The Vineland Adaptive Behavior Scales, Second Edition (Vineland – II).* Bloomington. MN: Pearson Assessments.

Strain, P. S. (1983). Generalization of autistic children's social behavior change: Effects of developmentally integrated and segregated settings. *Analysis and Intervention in Developmental Disabilities, 3,* 23-34.

Strain, P. S., Kerr, M. M., & Ragland, E. U. (1979). Effects of peer-mediated social initiations and prompting/reinforcement procedures on the social behavior of autistic children. *Journal of Autism and Developmental Disorders, 9,* 41-54.

Sundberg, M. L., & Partington, J. W. (1998). *Teaching language to children with autism or other developmental disabilities.* Pleasant Hill, CA: Behavior Analysts Inc.

Terrace, H. (1963). Discrimination learning with and without errors. *Journal of the Experimental Analysis of Behavior, 6*, 1-27.

Thompson, M. (1996.) *Andy and his yellow frisbee.* Bethesda, MD: Woodbine House.

Thorndike, R. L., Hagen, E. P., & Sattler, J. M. (1986). *Stanford-Binet Intelligence Scale – Fourth Edition.* Chicago: Riverside Publishing.

Touchette, P. E., & Howard, J. (1984). Errorless learning: Reinforcement contingencies and stimulus control transfer in delayed prompting. *Journal of Applied Behavior Analysis, 17*, 175-181.

Twatchman-Cullen, D. (2000). *How to be a para pro: A comprehensive training manual for paraprofessionals.* Higganum, CT: Starfish Specialty Press.

Wagner, S. (1999). *Inclusive programming for elementary students with autism.* Arlington, TX: Future Horizons.

Wechsler, D. (1989). *Wechsler Preschool and Primary Scale of Intelligence – Revised.* San Antonio, TX: The Psychological Corporation.

Wechsler, D. (1991). *Wechsler Intelligence Scale for Children – Third Edition.* San Antonio, TX: The Psychological Corporation.

Weiss, M. J. (2005). Comprehensive ABA Programs: integrating and evaluating the implementation of varied instructional approaches. *The Behavior Analyst Today, 6*, 249-256.

Weiss, M. J. (2001). Expanding ABA intervention in intensive programs for children with autism: The inclusion of Natural Environment training and Fluency Based Instruction. *The Behavior Analyst Today, 2*, 182-186.

Weiss, M. J., & Harris, S. L. (2001). *Reaching out, joining in: Teaching social skills to young children with autism.* Bethesda, MD: Woodbine House.

Whalen, C., & Schreibman, L. (2003). Joint attention training for children with autism using behavior modification procedures. *Journal of Child Psychology and Psychiatry & Allied Disciplines, 44,* 456-468.

Wolfberg, P. J. (2003). *Peer play and the autism spectrum: The art of guiding children's socialization and imagination.* Shawnee Mission, KS: Autism Asperger Publishing Company.

Zercher, C., Hunt, P., Schuler, A., & Webster, J. (2001). Increasing joint attention, play, and language through peer supported play. *Autism, 5,* 374-398.

INDEX

AAPC'S EXCLUSIVE PRACTICAL SOLUTIONS SERIES

Asperger Syndrome and Difficult Moments: Practical Solutions for Tantrums, Rage, and Meltdowns (Revised and Expanded Edition)

Brenda Smith Myles and Jack Southwick

Code 9901B   Price: $21.95
Code 9720 (DVD)   Price: $29.95

The Hidden Curriculum: Practical Solutions for Understanding Unstated Rules in Social Situations

Brenda Smith Myles, Melissa L. Trautman, and Ronda L. Schelvan

Code 9942 (book)   Price: $19.95
Code 9721 (DVD)   Price: $29.95
Code 9986 (2008 calendar)   Price: $15.95

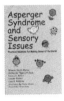

Asperger Syndrome and Sensory Issues: Practical Solutions for Making Sense of the World

Brenda Smith Myles, Katherine Tapscott Cook, Nancy E. Miller, Louann Rinner, and Lisa A. Robbins

Code 9907A   Price: $21.95

Perfect Targets: Asperger Syndrome and Bullying; Practical Solutions for Surviving the Social World

Rebekah Heinrichs

Code 9918   Price: $21.95

Asperger Syndrome and Adolescence: Practical Solutions for School Success

Brenda Smith Myles, Ph.D., and Diane Adreon

Code 9908   Price: $23.95

Finding Our Way: Practical Solutions for Creating a Supportive Home and Community for the Asperger Syndrome Family

Kristi Sakai

Code 9948   Price: $21.95

Asperger Syndrome and the Elementary School Experience: Practical Solutions for Academic & Social Difficulties

Susan Thompson Moore

Code 9911   Price: $23.95

Practical Solutions for Educating Young Children with High-Functioning Autism and Asperger Syndrome

Mary Jane Weiss, Ph.D.

Code 9003   Price: $21.95

Practical Solutions to Everyday Challenges for Children with Asperger Syndrome

Haley Morgan Myles

Code 9917   Price: $12.95

Girls Under the Umbrella of Autism Spectrum Disorders: Practical Solutions for Addressing Everyday Challenges

Lori Ernsperger, Ph.D., and Danielle Wendel

Code 9989   Price: $19.95

Place your order online at www.asperger.net, or call toll-free: 877-AS Publish (877-277-8254)

A̸PC

Autism Asperger Publishing Company
P.O. Box 23173
Shawnee Mission, Kansas 66283-0173
877-277-8254
www.asperger.net